More than Rubies

Becoming a Woman of Godly Influence

Debra White Smith

Beacon Hill Press of Kansas City
Kansas City, Missouri

Library of Congress Cataloging-in-Publication Data

Smith, Debra White.
    More than rubies : becoming a woman of Godly influence / Debra White Smith.
        p. cm.
    Includes bibliographical references.
    ISBN 0-8341-1813-0 (pbk)
        1. Wives—Religious life. 2. Mothers—Religious life. I. Title.

    BV4528.15 .S65 2000
    248.8'43—dc21

                                                                99-057993

10   9   8   7   6   5   4   3   2   1

To my mother

Contents

A wife of noble character who can find?
She is worth far more than rubies.
Her husband has full confidence in her
and lacks nothing of value.
She brings him good, not harm,
all the days of her life.
She selects wool and flax
and works with eager hands.
She is like the merchant ships,
bringing her food from afar.
She gets up while it is still dark;
she provides food for her family
and portions for her servant girls.
She considers a field and buys it;
out of her earnings she plants a vineyard.
She sets about her work vigorously;
her arms are strong for her tasks.
She sees that her trading is profitable,
and her lamp does not go out at night.
In her hand she holds the distaff
and grasps the spindle with her fingers.
She opens her arms to the poor
and extends her hands to the needy.
When it snows, she has no fear for her household;
for all of them are clothed in scarlet.
She makes coverings for her bed;
she is clothed in fine linen and purple.
Her husband is respected at the city gate,
where he takes his seat among the elders of the land.
She makes linen garments and sells them,
and supplies the merchants with sashes.
She is clothed with strength and dignity;
she can laugh at the days to come.

She speaks with wisdom,
and faithful instruction is on her tongue.
She watches over the affairs of her household
and does not eat the bread of idleness.
Her children arise and call her blessed;
her husband also, and he praises her:
"Many women do noble things,
but you surpass them all."
Charm is deceptive, and beauty is fleeting;
but a woman who fears the LORD is to be praised.
Give her the reward she has earned,
and let her works bring her praise at the city gate.

—Prov. 31:10-31

Preface

The Inspiration for This Book

When I was 15, my mother was diagnosed with manic depressive disorder. Later that diagnosis was changed to schizophrenia. She had been a pastor's wife, a children's evangelist, and a spiritual inspiration to many around her. Yet she lost her mind. My parents divorced when I was 17. When I was 24, I obtained protective custody of my mentally ill mother, and at the release of this book I have had custody of her for 12 years. Currently she resides in a foster home for adults in a nearby town. Heavily sedated, her days blur into each other as she sits, watches television, and sleeps.

That's a rather mild description of a 20-year horror story for me. For the first 15 of those 20 years, I felt as if I had undergone an emotional abortion—torn asunder, bloody, destroyed. This tragedy, mixed with issues of sexual abuse, produced times that I would have gladly embraced death.

But at long last, God began a healing miracle in me. When I became really serious with Him and started "panting" after Him "as the deer pants for streams of water" (Ps. 42:1), God began to heal me. And with that healing came a powerful awareness of the influence a wife and mother has on her family, of the tragedy our family underwent at the "loss" of my mother, of the devastation any family feels when robbed of motherly influence for whatever reason. But I also began to see what a tragedy it is when wives and mothers don't comprehend just how influential they really are.

After this awareness enveloped me, I began to notice the many women who never tap into the spiritual truths God sets before them in Scripture. Consequently, they never impact their families to the level God intends. We often go through our lives attending church, smiling in public, saying all the right things, and putting on a good picture when in reality we're far from the spiritual powerhouses God desires us to be. As godly women, our first calling is to the daily, determined pursuit of all that He deems holy.

Therefore, being an effective Christian wife and mother is not just about getting the family into church. That duty is extremely important, of course. But whether a woman is 20 or 70, being a Christian wife and mother is more about being a vehicle through which God can permeate every corner of the home.

Promise Keepers has awakened a nation of men to their role as the spiritual leaders in our homes. That thrills me. However, it's time for women to deeply realize that they have an equally important spiritual role in the home and truly see the tremendous impact God intends them to have on their families. My intent is to challenge, to inform, and to inspire. Because of the experiences with my own mother, *More than Rubies* has been 20 years in the making. And I'm convinced that if every Christian woman in America would implement the truths in these pages, we would experience a spiritual revolution—a revival in our homes, our churches, and our marriages that would shake the universe!

In His Service,
Debra White Smith

Acknowledgments

This book would not exist without some really great men:
    First, Daniel, my husband. Thanks, Daniel, for being such a support to my writing.
    Second, Gaylon White, my father, for doing the best he could when my mother could no longer be there.
    Third, Kelly Gallagher, director of Beacon Hill Press of Kansas City. Thanks, Kelly, for being open to God's voice.
    Fourth, Bruce Nuffer, product development editor for Beacon Hill Press of Kansas City. Thanks, Bruce, for graciously bumping my deadline.
    Fifth, my critique partner, Bob Osborne. Thanks, Bob, for telling me that if I didn't use my thesaurus, you were going to strangle me. You're so thoughtful!

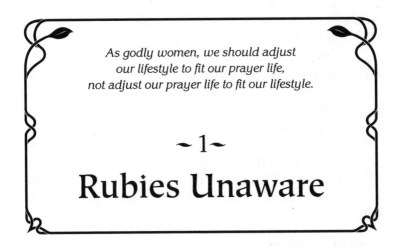

~1~

Rubies Unaware

"The wife is the spirit of the home."
"The hand that rocks the cradle rules the world."
"Beside every successful man is a great woman."
"When Mama ain't happy, ain't nobody happy!"

These clichés have been passed from one generation to the next and are actually true. You really *are* the spirit of your home. Your role as a mother *does* determine how the world is and will be ruled. You *are* a key factor in deciding the success of your husband. And *your* happiness, or lack of it, *does* determine the happiness of your family.

Consider Solomon, the wisest man in history. In spite of his wisdom and powerful relationship with God, his wives led him to worship false gods (see 1 Kings 11). Solomon's spiritual demise reveals a potent example of a wife's influence. Unlike King Solomon's pagan consorts, God wants Christian wives and mothers to guide their families toward a deeper walk with Him. However, it seems that many women are actually unaware of the powerful influence they exude in their homes. Do you understand just how persuasive you are? According to a recent study by Barna Research Group, 78 percent of teens say their parents, and especially their mothers, have considerable influence in their thinking and behavior.[1]

Danni was a young woman who didn't grasp just how influential she really was. She went through life doing the normal things a Christian wife and mother does without fully realizing the spiritual impact, or lack of spiritual impact in some cases, that she was having on her family. Danni could be you or me or any Christian woman across America who spends her life focused on what society dictates rather than what God's Word urges. From Danni's story begin your own journey toward an awakening of your spiritual influence.

▷ Danni's Story

A good wife and mother, a dedicated Christian, a committed church member, an asset to her community and her family—Danni was all of these things. But one thing dissatisfied her about her home; her husband didn't seem to carry out his role as spiritual leader. Even though Brice was dedicated to church and seemed dedicated to God, he seldom took initiative in the home concerning spiritual matters. For years Danni prayed that Brice would recognize what she thought was completely his responsibility in their home.

At long last Brice joined a Christian men's group. His decision made Danni's heart sing. She took pride in his new T-shirts with Bible verses on them. But she soon realized the only change was more laundry.

Occasionally Danni thought about starting a Bible study with her husband and a prayer time with her kids, which could perhaps create a deeper spiritual atmosphere in her home. In spite of her conscience's nudging, she stubbornly clung to the concept that the spirituality of her home was completely Brice's job. She inwardly insisted that he be the one to do it, but Brice failed to see the need.

When the children entered school, Danni finally quit praying about the spirituality of her home. After years of frustration, giving up was easy. She decided that church on

Sunday would have to be enough and hoped for the best with her children.

Unaware

Does Danni sound familiar? Is it a bit too close to home? Few honest women say that they think their husbands are doing everything they should to fulfill their God-given call as their home's spiritual leader. I believe that in some instances this comes from misplaced expectations. Many times we expect our husbands to do what God has called *us* to do. We don't understand that our husbands cannot and will not fulfill every spiritual role within our homes.

God's plan is different. Husbands are to be the leader of a two-party team, and a leader working alone without team effort accomplishes precious little. On a football team the quarterback is the leader, but a quarterback without a team is essentially powerless. Each team member has a role, and each role is important to the winning of the game. The same is true of a husband-wife team when developing the spirituality of a home.

Several years ago I heard a Christian talk show about men as spiritual leaders. Several despairing women called in to talk to the nationally recognized male guest about what they could do to get their husbands to be the spiritual leaders in their homes. One particularly distraught woman was a pastor's wife. She said of her husband, "He leads the whole church, but he won't initiate our family prayer time."

Like Danni, I believe that some of those women were thinking they had a lesser role in the spirituality of their homes: "I'm just a wife . . . just a mother . . . just a woman. Obviously my spiritual responsibilities in my home aren't as important as my husband's. The Bible says that 'the husband is the head of the wife,' the leader of the home. So the spiritual responsibility of our family rests squarely on his shoulders."

Even if wives verbally disagree with this statement, the idea often permeates their actions and attitudes. While they focus on their husband's lack of spirituality in the home, they lose sight of Eph. 5, which clearly states the responsibility of spiritual leadership of the family does not rest totally with the husband.

With the revival of men becoming aware of their spiritual leadership roles in the family, women sometimes act as if they're off the hook: "Now that my husband has awakened to his leadership role, I can step back and cruise through this family spirituality thing a little more easily." When the husband fails to do it all, then the wife becomes frustrated and, like Danni, disillusioned. Many give up.

The wife must see herself as an element as vital in the spirituality of the home as is her husband. Although their roles are different, they are equally important. Homes desperately need both. An irony of the modern feminist movement is that the participants have bought into the very thought process they are fighting—a mind-set of the belief that you are important only if you fulfill a man's role. So in an attempt to feel important, many feminists encourage women to take the roles of men. The problem is that it actually reinforces the very chauvinism it claims to fight by telling women that they can't achieve success or importance until society accepts them in a man's role. In truth, a wife and mother is the most important when she strives to fulfill her own God-created spiritual role. Likewise, a man is the most important when he strives to fulfill his own God-created spiritual role, not when he's out conquering corporate America. Together, these divergent but equal roles deliver a powerful and influential punch in our society, our homes, and future generations.

The husband is to ooze sacrificial love in every corridor of his home and then be the first one to exemplify the truths found in the Word of God (Eph. 5:23-26). Like Christ, the husband should also sacrifice himself for his wife and family; he should guide and protect. These are not the wife's responsibilities—they're the husband's.

The wife's spiritual role to her family seems a bit blur-ry to women like Danni, but any woman who passively awaits her husband to carry out every spiritual role in the home should contemplate the multi-faceted role of the Church. (See Matt. 9:15; 25:1-13; Mark 2:19-20.) One of its primary roles is to create a godly, worshipful atmosphere within its walls and in the world. Similarly, creating a spirit of worship, a godly atmosphere, in the home is one of the wife's primary spiritual roles.

Prov. 31:27 says, "She watches over the affairs of her household." This suggests that most women have their fingertips on the domestic "pulse" of the home. If our spiritual role in the home is to be fulfilled, the first thing we need to be busy doing is what the Church does. Our very first concern should be for spiritual matters, not whether the carpet received its regular shampoo.

▷ Danni's Story

One day when her little ones had grown into adolescents, Danni began to panic about her family's lack of spirituality. True, she had given up on Brice leading in family devotions when her kids were small. But now her son and daughter were older and facing who-knew-what out in the real world. Danni began having visions of her children emerging into adulthood without so much as one memory of a family altar time. She also began to despair that the children probably wouldn't begin a family prayer time when they got married. Brice, still a caring Christian, certainly had blown it in fulfilling this aspect of his duty.

Upon contemplating Brice's failure in this regard, Danni had the same thought that had nagged her 10 years before when she gave up on her family's spirituality: What about *her* spiritual role in the home? Had she been to her family what God had called *her* to be? Soon Danni became deeply troubled as she began to realize the horrid truth: while she had wasted years standing around waiting on Brice to do *his* "job," *she* had a job that needed to be done. The spiritual burden did not rest wholly on Brice.

At once an agonizing hunger swept over Danni to see her family on their knees together. She began to wonder what would happen if she initiated the family altar time. So she tried it. Even though the kids protested a bit, Brice immediately agreed with her and even took the lead in prayer! She was so astounded that she could hardly pray herself. Danni felt an awareness that she had stumbled upon some truth, but she wasn't certain what it was.

Initiating Is Not Leading

Aside from having a thriving personal prayer time, one of the most important steps in creating a godly atmosphere in the home is regular prayer and Bible reading with the family and one-on-one with your spouse. This creates a bond of worship among family members and often leads to sharing prayer requests as well as spiritual struggles with the people to whom we live the closest. No other activity will knit your family together like prayer and Bible reading. Even if the children are grown and on their own, when they come home for visits, prayer and Bible reading should be an integral part of your family time. The length of family devotions depends upon the age of the children involved. The younger the children, the shorter the prayer time.

If extracurricular activities so cram your family's schedule that you don't have time to pray and read the Bible together, then cut back on those extracurricular activities. As godly women, we should adjust our lifestyle to fit our prayer life, not adjust our prayer life to fit our lifestyle. No music lessons or sports practice will create as well-rounded a child or grandchild as family devotions. Spending time with God is the most important element in your family's life. Sadly, a lot of churchgoing families never pray together except at mealtime because no one initiates it.

According to Webster, the word *initiate* means "to cause to begin." It does not mean to lead. For instance, let's say you discover your car has a flat tire when you go out to your garage in the morning. You tell your husband,

and he immediately takes the leadership role in changing
the tire. While you initiated the project by making your
husband aware of the need, you never once stood over him
and dictated how he should do it. You weren't the "leader"
in getting the tire changed; rather, you were the *initiator.* If
your husband won't initiate a family prayer time or prayer
as a couple, God will help you do it.

The most important thing is that family prayer happens.

There are some men who are very strong in areas of
spiritual leadership, such as making sure the family at-
tends church, enforcing biblical discipline and principles
with the children or grandchildren, setting a Christlike example, or showing sacrificial love. But sometimes these
same men seem unaware of the power of a family on its
knees. In these cases, it's perfectly appropriate for a wife
to initiate prayer. If after the wife initiates the family prayer
the husband still refuses to take the lead for whatever reason, the wife has no choice but to lead. Leading is not the
wife's role. Be careful that you don't automatically seize
this privilege from your husband based on faulty misconceptions about his willingness to lead. But if he absolutely
will not lead and you want to raise godly children and
grandchildren, somebody must teach them to seek God!

Any prayer is better than no prayer.

Sometimes husbands don't initiate family prayer time
because they process information different from women. In
his book *Love Is a Decision,* Gary Smalley uses a battleship
to illustrate how men and women think. "A woman's mind
is like the war room on a battleship. It's the nerve center,
equipped with fancy electronic devices that allow it to
monitor all the vital signs on every deck of the house at the
same time." Therefore women soak up every detail of their
surroundings. Men, on the other hand, tend to focus on
where they are and what they are doing. If they are on the
top deck of the battleship, they don't think about what
happened on the bottom deck or what might happen in the
control room. They're on the top deck. They think only

"top deck" thoughts. Women simultaneously think about the top deck, bottom deck, control room, and captain's quarters.[2]

Neither the male nor female type of thinking is superior to the other. We need both mind-sets to survive. I've often been immeasurably thankful that my husband is focused when I'm allowing the past or future to cloud my "now." By the same token, he has been thankful that I remind him what's about to happen in the control room when he's still thinking "top deck."

The point is that sometimes husbands don't think about a family prayer time simply because they're focused on "now." But if that prayer time is initiated, many godly men are more than willing to focus solely upon God and lead the family in spiritual concerns.

Equally important to God is the joint prayer of spouses. Once again, if your husband won't initiate the prayer time, then you initiate it. This time of communion and sharing does not have to be excessively long and most likely won't be long in the beginning. Even five minutes of prayer in the morning, standing in the dining room holding hands, is better than no prayer. God does not have a "prayer meter" that registers the length of your conversations with Him. You'll find that any time spent with Him will deepen your intimacy with your spouse and create a more godly atmosphere in the home. You'll also find that after you start consistently praying and sharing your spiritual journey with your spouse, you'll naturally fall into more lengthy prayer and sharing times.

If your husband absolutely refuses to pray with you, intercede on his behalf and remain silent to let God do His work. However, I believe there are few husbands, even non-Christians, who refuse a smiling, sincere wife's request for a quick prayer before the day starts. If your husband is one of those few, then don't underestimate the supernatural effects of prayer. Consistently pray that he will be open to prayer, and one day both God and your husband will surprise you. Never give up!

▷ Danni's Story

After Danni realized these truths, she initiated a family prayer time every night. Soon she saw that if she could start prayer with the whole family, perhaps she could also begin a private prayer time with Brice. Danni began to seek God about her spiritual role in her family. Gradually the Lord revealed to her the powerful spiritual influence she held in her family, an influence she had tried to thrust onto Brice. She opened her heart and allowed God to begin working on her, deciding to make the best of the years she had left with her children. In short, Danni started learning to "be the Church" to her family. She became "busy at home," not necessarily scrubbing the walls, but doing everything in her power to create a godly atmosphere.

Casanova and Oswald Chambers

What are your expectations for your husband? Do you see yourself in Danni? In all honesty, I see myself to some degree. Sometimes I think we want our husbands to arrive at the front door with a love sonnet and a bouquet of roses in one hand and a Bible in the other, equipped to share in a time of meaningful devotion. It's as though we want them to be a cross between Casanova and Oswald Chambers.

Guess what—that won't ever happen. Our husbands are not and can never fill such shoes. They're the spiritual leaders of our home, but we as wives have an equally weighty responsibility—creating a godly atmosphere in the home.

Only by a thorough understanding of the powerful influence we exert in our homes can women radically impact their families from one generation to the next. The time has come for that to happen in families! God himself told Moses, "[I show] love to a thousand generations of those who love me and keep my commandments" (Exod. 20:6). Do you know how to ensure that your family will see God's love for generations to come? Serve Him yourself, and allow His presence to permeate every corner of your home through you. There is amazing strength in a woman who is God-focused. Her household adopts the same focus. No force on earth can prevail against such strength.

Consider strong women from the Bible such as Hannah, who released her small son, Samuel, to the service of God; Ruth, who did what was honorable and stayed with her mother-in-law even in the face of the socially acceptable search for another husband; and Mary, the mother of our Lord and Savior. None of these women took their influence lightly. Each of them impacted their worlds for God and therefore saw God impact their lives. This combination is undeniably powerful.

A Special Message for Single Moms

My friend Freida married a man she was at total peace about. They had two girls born to them. Eventually the marriage failed, and the couple divorced. Freida, truly a woman of God, wanted to do what was absolutely right, so she remarried her ex-husband. Because of serious problems, the marriage failed again. When her two daughters were still in elementary school, Freida's ex-husband died. Not only was Freida now a single mom, but the girls no longer had their father's influence. Furthermore, Freida never remarried.

First fact of life: If Freida and her girls wanted to eat and to wear clothing, Freida had to work full-time. She had absolutely no choice.

First fact of God's grace: Even though she didn't have a formal college degree, God provided Freida with a wonderful job at a substantial salary that nicely supported her and her girls.

Second fact of life: Freida had to fill both the husband's and wife's roles of spiritual leadership for her family.

Second fact of God's grace: God provided Freida's daughters with a wonderful, strong male role model.

Third fact of life: Without the influence of a godly father, the girls stood the good chance of having poor self-esteem and becoming "loose" morally in an attempt to gain male attention.

Third fact of God's grace: Both girls successfully graduated from high school and attended college while dating little and remaining pure. Now in their mid-20s, they have both married solid Christian men.

My point? Sometimes life throws us some really nasty curveballs. Therefore, there are times when our lives don't perfectly line up with the pattern set in the Word of God because of choices made for us by those who were influenced by Satan. This can hurl us into a situation that we don't care to be in, such as trying to raise children as a single mother.

If you're a single mother, take heart from Freida's story. Realize that even if you're a widow or divorced, God's grace is still available for your situation. As it did with Freida, that grace can fill the gaps, or should I say, gaping holes, left in your life. The truths in this book still apply to you. Even if there's no husband in your household, God will honor your obedience to His Word, and in His grace He will provide for you, as He did my friend.

A wife of noble character who can find?
She is worth far more than rubies.
Her husband has full confidence in her
and lacks nothing of value.
She brings him good, not harm,
all the days of her life.

 —Prov. 31:10-12

Ruby "Am I's"

1. Am I expecting my husband to be responsible for my role to create a godly atmosphere in the home?

   Evidence that you are: You passively await your hus-

band to take care of every facet of your family's spirituality.

2. Am I trying to take over my husband's role as the spiritual leader in my home?
   Evidence that you are: You immediately jump in without giving your husband the chance to lead.

3. Am I praying for God's guidance in carrying out my
   spiritual role in my home?
   Evidence that you are: You are continually seeking
   ways to create a godly atmosphere.

4. Am I open to God's correction where I have failed?
   Evidence that you are: During your personal prayer
   time, you submit to God's purging rather than arguing
   with Him about how you were right.

5. Am I focused on God instead of what I perceive as my
   husband's lack of fulfilling his biblical role?
   Evidence that you are: You lack a continual mental ac-
   cusatory attitude toward your husband and focus on
   how to improve your own fulfillment of your biblical
   role.

Ruby "Ifs"

1. If your husband won't participate in family devotions but your children will:

- Make family devotions a regular routine with children of all ages.
- Plan them when your husband is away so that he won't feel left out or isolated.
- Don't make a point out of your husband's absence to him or to the children.
- As a family, earnestly seek *God* to change your husband's heart.
- Remember that it is not your job to change his heart.

2. If your children don't want to participate in family worship but your husband does:

- Include them in worship anyway, if they are still at home.
- Don't force high schoolers who refuse to worship since that might only heighten their resentment and harden them all the more to the voice of God.
- Intercede for God to place the desire in their hearts to participate in family prayer time.
- Make a point to pray with your spouse that God will change their hearts.
- Continue to offer them the opportunity to worship as a family, but if and when they refuse, drop the subject and continue to pray for them.

3. If your children and husband refuse to worship with you:

- Get on your face before God and ask Him to do what you can't—change their hearts.
- Don't try to nag them into it—that only aggravates the problem.
- Several times a year, give your family a chance to pray with you. A gentle "Would you like to pray with me tonight?" is always appropriate.

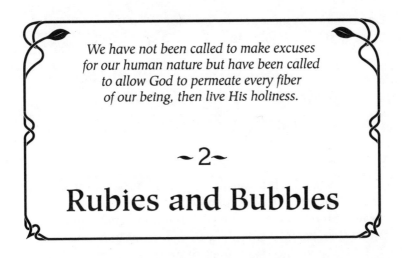

*We have not been called to make excuses
for our human nature but have been called
to allow God to permeate every fiber
of our being, then live His holiness.*

~2~

Rubies and Bubbles

Danni did quite well for a few months. Her family prayed and read the Bible together almost every night. She and Brice shared prayer and Bible reading quite often as well, and Danni felt more confident in being "worth more than rubies" than she ever had before. However, she began to notice a current of some undeniable negative force in her home that she never before encountered. Besides having family devotions, nothing had really changed in her household. Perhaps that was part of the problem.

Now that Danni was on her knees with her family and therefore more open to God, He began to show her an area in her life where she was actually destroying the godly atmosphere in her home. You see, Danni was a complainer, a criticizer, often demonstrated a less-than-godly attitude, and was involved in unresolved interpersonal conflicts from time to time. For years, Danni had excused her behavior as just being human and rationalized that all human beings complain, criticize, have bad attitudes, and don't get along with others.

Then God began to show Danni that she should try to be like Him, not excuse herself based on others. In her soul,

Danni felt as if she were stunned for a few days. Changing these habits was going to be one big spiritual struggle.

> *Set a guard over my mouth, O LORD;*
> *keep watch over the door of my lips.*
> —Ps. 141:3

Repeating Critical Patterns

Some of the first killers of a godly atmosphere are habitual criticizing and complaining, a bad attitude, and unresolved interpersonal conflicts. It seems women are more prone than men to grapple with sins of attitude and conflict. You may find that you're more detail-oriented than your husband. You also probably have a good memory. I believe this is a product of the feminine thought process that Gary Smalley defines as being "like a war room of a battleship." Since most of us miss nothing in our environments, we are often tempted to find plenty to criticize and complain about. This often leads to interpersonal conflicts, both in the home and out. If this were not a problem with women, Paul would not have written to Titus, "Teach the older women to be reverent in the way they live, not to be slanderers" (Titus 2:3). Slandering or criticizing and complaining often lead to an ungodly attitude and conflicts.

Think about your words as bubbles. Every time a word leaves your mouth, it's a bubble. That bubble is filled with one of two things, either slime or shine. These bubbles leave our mouths, float around the room, and land on the heads of our family, on our furniture, on the walls, in the bedrooms, in the bathrooms, and even in our yards. The bubbles then do what all bubbles do: they pop. What's inside clings to the spot where the bubble popped. If you criticize and complain, regularly exhibit a bad attitude, or expound on a conflict in process, then those bubbles are full of slime—green, mucky, stinky slime. That slime clings to every person in your household and seems to permeate

even the walls and yard. It stinks. It dries. It lays the foun-
dation for the next layer of slime. It inhibits spiritual, mental, and emotional growth. It spreads to everyone your
household encounters, like a bad case of poison ivy.

Some say, "Criticism is just a natural, human instinct"
and "Everyone complains and has a bad attitude" and
"Who doesn't live from one conflict to the next?" Just because it's natural doesn't mean it's good. Poison ivy is natural. We are not called to make excuses for our human nature—we are called to allow God to permeate every fiber of
our being, then live His holiness.

In Romans, Paul states, "There is therefore now no
condemnation to those who are in Christ Jesus, who do not
walk according to the flesh, but according to the Spirit"
(8:1, NKJV). A woman who is walking according to the Spirit
receives no condemnation from God and likewise passes no
condemnation to others. In Phil. 2:14-15 Paul also writes,
"Do everything without complaining or arguing, so that you
may become blameless and pure, children of God without
fault in a crooked and depraved generation, in which you
shine like stars in the universe." When we as godly women
allow God's Spirit to truly purge what comes from our
mouths and our hearts, our "word bubbles" are filled with
praise, encouragement, and love—with shine instead of
slime. We'll know the blessings of the Lord. "How good and
pleasant it is when brothers [and sisters] live together in
unity! . . . For there the LORD bestows his blessing, even life
forevermore" (Ps. 133:1, 3). We will "shine like stars in the
universe" and reflect the glory of God himself.

Shine explodes from those bubbles to spread a glow
on every person and item it encounters. Your children
and/or grandchildren will shine. Your husband will shine.
The furniture and yard and everything those word bubbles
pop on will shine. It's like contagious laughter that spreads
to everyone your household touches.

The result? Your whole family will see you in a new light.
The atmosphere of your home will shine. *You* will shine.

▷ Danni's Story

As Danni struggled with stopping her criticizing, complaining, and bad attitudes, she reflected on her mother and father during her own childhood. Danni remembered that they habitually criticized neighbors, relatives, or church members. She recalled how her father never seemed free of complaints about the weather or the dinner or the noise Danni and her brother made. Danni contemplated her mother's varying attitudes and the regular times those attitudes were indeed bad. She also mused over all the times her mother had been involved in conflicts at church.

One day Danni realized that she had grown up in a household full of slime bubbles. Those slime bubbles had been popping on Danni since birth. By the time she left home and married Brice, her spirit was covered in a very thick, dried layer of slime. Every word she spoke, every attitude she exhibited was forced to travel through that layer of stinky, thick slime before it emerged into her home. In other words, Danni's parents trained her to be a criticizer and complainer, to exhibit bad attitudes, and to instigate conflict simply by demonstrating that behavior in front of her.

Exod. 34:7 states that God "punishes the children and their children for the sin of the fathers to the third and fourth generation." As I understand this verse, it does not mean that God will punish me for a sin my father or mother committed, one that I did not myself commit. What it does mean, I believe, is that if there is unconfessed and unrepented sin in a parent's life, he or she will very likely teach his or her children by example how to continue in that sin. The children simply carry out the behavior that the parent demonstrates and then in turn teach their own children how to continue in that same sin. It's a cycle. But fortunately that cycle can be broken. That's what a relationship with Jesus Christ is all about—breaking the bondage of sin.

If we as wives and mothers are to be "worth far more than rubies," we must allow God to show us if our spirits are

covered in the slime from our parents, then ask Him to purify our hearts. Otherwise, we'll continue to react from our
past rather than from His righteousness. Only after we come
face-to-face with the way our thought patterns were affected
as children are we then able to ask God to purge us of criticizing, complaining, bad attitudes, and perpetual conflicts. In
1 Cor. 13:11 Paul states, "When I was a child, I talked like a
child, I thought like a child, I reasoned like a child. When I
became a man, I put childish ways behind me" (v. 11). In order to put the ways of childhood behind us, we first must
recognize them and also recognize their source.

It's very easy to be in denial at this point and say, "Oh,
my parents were saints," especially if your parents are no
longer living. But what does God say to you? Even if your
parents never criticized you or complained about you, did
they criticize people in front of you? Did they habitually
complain in the home? Did they regularly exhibit a negative
attitude for the whole household to see? Did they openly
fume about the latest conflict at church or elsewhere?

If the answer to any of those questions is yes, consider
yourself "slimed."

This isn't an exercise in pointing a finger at our parents and blaming them for our behavior. Regardless of
what our parents did or didn't do, it's still our responsibility
to recognize where we are inhibiting the godly atmosphere
of our homes and ask God to cleanse those areas of our
lives. Otherwise, we teach our children to "slime" their own
children.

Criticism and Truth

A lot of criticism is based in truth. We all have things
that are wrong with us—the downside of our personalities
or the areas in which we're still growing spiritually. It's very
easy to focus on the faults of our friends, relatives, and acquaintances rather than on their good points.

Criticism is a convenient way to divert attention from
personal downfalls. People who criticize usually feel inferior

to others. That's the whole point in criticizing. "If I can make everybody else look bad, then I feel superior," and this momentarily relieves the torture of inferiority. But as long as I'm focused on others' faults and criticizing them, I prohibit God from showing me my own faults. Criticism says nothing about the person being criticized. It says everything about the criticizer. The person who looks the worst in the end is the criticizer.

There is always someone to criticize. It takes very little effort.

If we're to have a godly impact on the atmosphere of our homes, we must abandon making critical issues out of small things. This doesn't mean that there isn't a time and place for "speaking the truth in love" (Eph. 4:15). But if you don't feel that the issue is something that she should be lovingly and tactfully confronted with, then don't share the tidbit with the rest of your family. We tend to think, "It won't hurt if I just tell my husband. He won't be affected." Oh, yes he will. You're responsible for the atmosphere in your home. Every critical remark you make leaves a slimy imprint on anyone you share it with. Whether we directly criticize our family or criticize others in front of our family, the slime is still there.

God is constantly working on all of us. None of us is free of areas where we don't need growth. We all have blind spots that God reveals to us in His time, when we have the spiritual maturity to deal with them. Danni, for instance, rocked along doing fine for a few months before God revealed the sin of criticism in her life. At that point, she became responsible for tapping into God's power to enable her to stop criticizing. There's never an excuse for a Christian woman to continue in a recognized sin that God has revealed to her. God reveals these areas to us so we'll repent, ask Him to cleanse us, and tap into His strength to avoid repeating the same sin.

When I fling open the door of my heart and radically abandon myself to God, He reveals those dark areas to me one by one. I have a choice: I can allow Him to remove the dark spot and purify me in that area or I can cling to the darkness and say, "But that's just the way I am. And that's the way my mother was before me." If I cling to the darkness of any one of those spots, then my clinging stops spiritual growth and prohibits God's moving to the next spot. Human beings have a tendency to cling to those dark spots because spot removal hurts. Don't ever think that God's purging is painless.

As long as I focus on what's wrong with everybody else, I prohibit God from showing me what's wrong with me.

Complaining Reveals Thanklessness

At the root of complaining is thanklessness. When we get our focus off God's blessings and onto our own demands, we start complaining. A complaining spirit is contagious. Usually if Mom complains about her family, the family will complain about Mom and each other. Our family is God's gift to us: "Sons are a heritage from the LORD, children a reward from him" (Ps. 127:3). When we complain about them—to their faces or behind their backs—we complain against God.

I'm not encouraging women to sweep real family problems under the rug and pretend they don't exist. But if there's a true problem within a marriage or family, habitual complaining, nagging, or even criticizing will never bring an end to that problem. The problem must be calmly and lovingly confronted and dealt with in a prayerful, biblical manner and according to the type of problem it is. Constant complaining and criticizing will only worsen the problem.

Prov. 27:15 states, "A quarrelsome [or complaining] wife is like a constant dripping on a rainy day." Think about how a drip affects you. It begins as an annoyance and eventually drives you nuts. You will either go to all lengths to stop the drip or train your ears to adapt to the noise and ignore it.

Suppose your ceiling is leaking in your living room, and you place a metal container beneath the leak to catch the water. After three days of heavy rain, you learn to stop listening to that drip. Even though the drip increases, you still have so trained your ears not to hear the leak that you don't realize you have a serious problem in the living room. When the ceiling caves, you're astounded.

The same holds true in families. After years of listening to Mom's complaining, a family will eventually tune out everything she says. Even if the concern she has is important, the family will ignore it because of Mom's track record. The only thing that will remain of the complaining is a lasting imprint of the behavior. Like the water rings left on a ceiling after a leak, complaining leaves its imprint on a family. The husband and/or children will daily enter the world with a new layer of slime.

> *One of the things a habitual complainer often says is "Life isn't fair." Truthfully, life really isn't fair. God has blessed* *each of us more than we ever deserved.*

When I'm tempted to complain, I ask myself five questions:

1. **Do I have clean water to drink?**
2. **Do I have plenty to eat?**
3. **Are my family and I relatively healthy?**
4. **Do I have adequate medical care?**
5. **Do I have at least two changes of clothing, a car, and a clean place in which to live?**

Answering yes to these questions forces me to realize that my lifestyle greatly exceeds that of the vast majority of the world. And even if the food at the restaurant last night wasn't particularly tasty, I remind myself that I'm not dying of hunger in some remote corner of the world, I don't have to beg in order to get food and clothing, and I don't have to search for tonight's protective shelter for my children.

If you can openly worship Christ, be thankful.

If you have arms, be thankful.

If you have a good home for your children, be thankful.

If you can walk, be thankful.

Bad Attitudes

An attitude is like the fire of our soul. And every day we get to choose the fuel for our fire. If our fuel consists of God's joy, peace, and love, then we put forth a pleasing aroma of righteousness, which blesses our family and all who encounter us. If our fuel is of anger, bitterness, or self-ishness, then we put forth an irritating smoke that invades our homes and chokes the spiritual life out of our family.

Attitude is a choice. There is always—absolutely always—something in our lives about which we can develop a bad attitude: This didn't get done right; that person reacted wrong; the house is always a wreck, no matter how much we clean it. When we fuel our emotions with these types of thoughts, our attitudes will grow out of proportion, filling our homes with a smoke so thick that family members must grope to find their emotional and spiritual stability.

According to John Maxwell's *The Winning Attitude,* "Two things must be stated to emphasize the power of our thought life. Major premise: We can control our thoughts. Minor premise: Our feelings come from our thoughts. Con-clusion? We can control our feelings by learning to change one thing: the way we think. . . . Our thought life, not our circumstances, determines our happiness."[1]

Bad attitudes are an immature way to focus the whole family on "me." As long as I'm brooding, the rest of the household must adjust to me and cater to my whims. The more the family asks, "What's wrong, Mom?" the more we can say something like "Nothing—just nothing. Just leave me alone." That creates an even greater focus on ourselves and destroys any hope for a Christ-centered home, for the home will be centered on a bad attitude.

Conflicts

There's always somebody with whom to be at odds. There's always a conflict to be had. As godly women, we can *choose* not to participate when a conflict is underway. Most of the time, participation in interpersonal conflict is a *choice*. Even if a person verbally attacks you, you do not have to heatedly defend yourself. Instead, you can *choose* to follow biblical principles and watch the potential conflicts dissolve to nothing. As the atmosphere "thermometer" in the home, godly women can choose not to involve themselves in petty arguments. These squabbles can be with other women or men, our husbands, or our children—especially if they're grown. Even if an argument occurs outside the home, it greatly affects the home's atmosphere, because we carry the anxiety with us and often discuss the problem with our family. If we're to create a godly atmosphere in our homes, there must come a point in our Christian maturity when we return good for evil and refuse to participate in petty personality conflicts and arguments.

Understand that there will be times when we must stand for truth as Jesus did when He cleared the Temple of the money changers (see Mark 11:15-17). Found in a similar situation, our stance for truth might likewise cause anger. At these times, the conflict is not with us; it's with truth. And the only way we can resolve the conflict will be to change truth. Jesus Christ never changed truth to accommodate feelings. But be careful not to lump all conflicts into this category and self-righteously think something like "Well, I was just telling the truth to her face, so I'm off the hook." All the times Jesus Christ became angry, His anger was related to the injustice dealt others, not himself. His anger was pure, righteous, and holy. Even when He was being crucified, He did not lash out to defend himself.

Quite frankly, I can become very angry when I think of

governments that deprive their citizens of the basic necessities of life for political purposes. I become very angry when I see destitute orphans who are rejected by potential adoptive parents because they are not physically perfect or not of a particular race. This anger is righteous. It does not involve the defense of me or my rights—it involves the defense of others.

The following verses actually outline ways to stop interpersonal conflicts before they start as well as to put an end to existing conflicts. Exercise them in all relationships, including those with your husband, children, and closest friends, and you'll find that the atmosphere of your home will be nothing short of a positive force.

1. *In everything, do to others what you would have them do to you, for this sums up the Law and the Prophets* (Matt. 7:12). Extend to everyone you know the same kindness, gentleness, respect, and love that you want to receive.

2. *Speaking the truth in love, we will in all things grow up into him who is the Head, that is, Christ* (Eph. 4:15). Even when the truth is negative, speak it with love, not with yelling, resentment, or hate.

3. *Do not let any unwholesome talk come out of your mouths, but only what is helpful for building others up according to their needs, that it may benefit those who listen. And do not grieve the Holy Spirit of God, with whom you were sealed for the day of redemption. Get rid of all bitterness, rage and anger, brawling and slander, along with every form of malice. Be kind and compassionate to one another, forgiving each other, just as in Christ God forgave you* (Eph. 4:29-32). Verse 29 gives the plan for never starting a conflict—speaking only words that will build others up. Verse 30 tells me that if I do start a conflict or am involved in a petty interpersonal conflict, it grieves the Holy Spirit. Verse 31 says I have no room in my life for conflict. Verse 32 says I have no room in my life for a lack of kindness, compassion, or forgiveness, even when I was the wronged party.

4. *You have heard that it was said, "You shall love your neighbor and hate your enemy." But I say to you, love your enemies, bless those who curse you, do good to those who hate you, and pray for those who spitefully use you and persecute you* (Matt. 5:43-44, NKJV). Even when I don't feel like it, I've found that if I do good to those who have wronged me, pray for them, and bless them, the love happens and the conflict dissolves. The equation for loving your enemy or the person you're in conflict with is this: blessing them plus doing good to them plus praying for them equals loving them.

In most cases there are three sides to interpersonal conflict: your side, their side, and the right side. Until everyone in such a conflict has responded in a thoroughly Christlike manner, there is no right side or wrong side. In other words, someone else's un-Christlike behavior never justifies my own un-Christlike behavior. This truth sheds new light on any conflict in which I have ever been involved. It forces me to examine my own behavior, stop pointing fingers, and make restitution—even if the other party refuses to. This truth also frees me from the necessity of taking sides when friends and acquaintances are involved in conflict. If we habitually participate in conflict, we grieve not only the Holy Spirit but also our families by "sliming" them and destroy any potential for a godly atmosphere in our homes.

> **Better to live on a corner of the roof**
> **than share a house with a quarrelsome wife.**
> (Prov. 21:9; 25:24)

On PMS

Isn't it great to be a female and enjoy the monthly benefit. Quite frankly, I'd rather be boiled in oil with a dozen rattlesnakes and a rabid Godzilla. But putting my opinions

aside, it's true that the female body's monthly cycle affects
the attitude, and for some women it's more drastic than for
others. Vitamins, extra rest, and eating right can help us
cope. (If that doesn't work, try solitary confinement.) All
joking aside, premenstrual syndrome (PMS) should never
be an excuse or a crutch. When we say something like "Oh,
well, I've got PMS—I'm entitled to a bad attitude or a tem-
per tantrum," then we're using our hormones as an excuse
to behave in an un-Christlike manner.

That doesn't mean I always want to tiptoe through the
tulips right before my starting date. Sometimes I'd rather
stomp through those tulips; sometimes I'd rather rip the
tulips up and sling them out of the yard. Nonetheless, what
I want to do on the inside and what I do on the outside isn't
always the same, especially if I'm focusing on God and asking Him to extend an extra dose of self-control that week.

Yes, there's supernatural help even for PMS. There's
also ibuprofen for pain and coffee to keep your limp brain
alert. Use them! (However, if your PMS has grown out of
control, resulting in rage and/or throwing things, you may
be experiencing a serious hormone imbalance that needs
medical treatment. I urge you, for the sake of your family,
to have the problem medically treated.)

Ruby Habits

Granted—we're all going to have bad days. If you experience a tragedy of any sort, you'll also experience depression. That's normal and healthy and, depending on the
extent of the tragedy, depression can overshadow your life
for a few weeks or even a few years. Furthermore, according to James Dobson in his book *What Wives Wish Their
Husbands Knew About Women,* most high moments in our
lives are also followed by down times, simply because of
the cycle of human emotions.[2]

During the writing of this book, I had the worst day in
my attempts to be a good mother. My two-year-old daughter had a case of "S&S"—sick and screaming. Because of

her illness, I was trying to survive three days on one-and-a-half night's sleep while tending to both her needs and the normal, regular needs of my four-year-old boy. By the end of the day, I was not a happy camper. When my husband came home that evening, I met him at the door and said, "I love you with my whole heart. I love our children with my whole heart. I love our home with my whole heart. But I'm going to take my Bible, get in the car, and probably won't be back for about an hour." I went for a walk and then sat in my car in the driveway with my Bible and some worship music.

If you have the flu or your child has the flu, you're going to be a bit grouchy and complain about lack of sleep. Otherwise we would be robots. But there's a vast difference between normal seasons of depression or occasional bad days and habitual bad days several times a week in which we allow ourselves to fall into negative behavioral patterns. God has not called us to a defeated lifestyle of one bad day after another. Complaining, criticizing, bad attitudes, and conflicts really are habit-forming. You usually can't stop with just one conflict, cutting comment, or complaint; and bad attitudes have a way of smoking up the whole room, not just your corner.

Throughout the Old Testament, the children of Israel fell into worshiping false gods such as Baal. God repeatedly became angry with them, probably because part of the worship ritual often included sacrificing children to Baal. Baal was thought of as "the god of storms," and the Israelites bought into the pagan belief that by slitting a child's throat, cremating him or her, and burying him or her in the walls of the temple, Baal would produce more rain. Other elements of Baal worship included interacting with temple prostitutes on what was referred to as "the high places."[3]

When we habitually complain about our family, we slit their throats emotionally and spiritually. When we repeatedly criticize them, we might as well be cremating their emotions and spirit. When we constantly smoke up the house with a nasty attitude, we might as well be burning incense to a false god—ourselves. If we live from one inter-personal conflict to the next in front of our families, we're doing nothing short of interacting with people who, like the temple prostitutes, have scorned the holy decrees of a holy God. And by our willing participation, we, too, are scorning our Creator. How, then, can we ever expect to influence our families for the holy God of Israel?

As godly women, we must be radically obedient in de-molishing every high place within our hearts. Otherwise, there is no chance that our families will ever see the Lord in us.

I don't struggle as much with habitual complaining or bad attitudes as I do with criticism and conflicts. These are my weak points, and Satan knows it. Occasionally there are times when someone will really get under my skin. Depend-ing on your personality type, your areas of struggle will vary. Or you might be like Danni and struggle with all four.

▷ Danni's Story

After a multitude of spiritual struggles, Danni finally got to a point where she stopped criticizing and complain-ing in front of her family. In other words, she learned to "bite her tongue." God even helped her stop exhibiting a bad attitude, and she saw a drastic reduction in the con-flicts in which she was involved. The atmosphere in her home seemed to improve greatly, but the atmosphere in Danni's mind didn't. You see, Danni had simply learned to control the outward manifestations of an inward problem. Soon she realized that even though she wasn't "sliming" her family, she was "sliming" herself. Would she ever grow past her need to bite her tongue, cover up her attitude, or avoid the people with whom she had been in conflict?

A wife of noble character who can find?
She is worth far more than rubies. . . .
She is clothed with strength and dignity;

she can laugh at the days to come.
She speaks with wisdom,
and faithful instruction is on her tongue.

—Prov. 31:10, 25-26

Ruby "Am I's"

1. Am I killing the godly atmosphere in my home with habitual criticism, complaining, conflicts, or a bad attitude?
      Evidence that you are: This chapter made you very un-
      comfortable and might have even irritated you.

2. Am I using criticism to cover my own faults?
      Evidence that you are: You usually criticize others in
      the very areas in which you struggle.

3. Am I complaining instead of being thankful?
      Evidence that you are: You talk about what's wrong in
      many situations rather than what's right.

4. Am I manifesting a bad attitude instead of the joy of the
   Lord?
      Evidence that you are: Your family members often ask
      you, "What's the matter?" or try to avoid you altogeth-
      er.

5. Am I living from one conflict to another?
      Evidence that you are: You think back on the last few
      years and remember a number of arguments you were
      involved in or arguments in which you blindly took
      sides.

6. Am I an adult survivor of childhood "slime"?
      Evidence that you are: Looking back on your child-
      hood, you recall bad times with predominant feelings of
      being "not good enough" or "a nuisance," or wondering
      what you did to make Mom [Dad] so grouchy.

7. Am I "sliming" myself?
      Evidence that you are: Your thought life doesn't match
      your family life. You might put on a good front with the
      family, but you think critically, complain in your head,

grumble under your breath, or simply hide conflicts from your family.

8. Am I using PMS or other physical burdens as an excuse for negative behavior?

Evidence that you are: You often say or think things like, "Well, I'm just acting this way because of my monthly cycle. I'm entitled!"

Ruby "Ifs"

1. **If you're a habitual complainer:**
   - Focus on what's good in your life rather than on what's wrong.
2. **If you habitually exhibit a bad attitude:**
   - Imagine your attitude as irritating smoke, choking the emotional and spiritual life out of your family.
3. **If you're a habitual criticizer:**
   - Think crooked underwear (ask yourself if you're being too judgmental).
4. **If you're habitually involved in conflicts:**
   - Accept the fact that in most interpersonal conflicts there are three sides: your side, their side, and the right side.
5. **If you have normal PMS:**
   - Eat right, get plenty of rest, take vitamins, and pray for self-control.
6. **If you have extreme PMS:**
   - Get medical attention.
7. **If your husband has PMS . . .**
   - OK, let's just say if your husband is a criticizer, is a complainer, is often involved in conflicts, or has a bad attitude, pray for him instead of responding with a complaint, a critical remark, or a bad attitude of your own.

> *We will never learn to control our thoughts and tongues and truly be what we need to be to our families unless we daily take time to encounter God in a radical way.*

~3~

Rubies and Fragrance

▷ Danni's Story

Danni began to realize that if she was going to stay spiritually victorious, she needed more than the prayer time with her husband and family. She desperately wanted to rid her mind of its critical bent, of its complaining, of its bad attitudes—but the more she tried the worse she failed. On one particularly horrible day, she threw herself face-down on her bed and poured her heart out to God. In a moment of abandonment, she relinquished all she was to her holy Creator and begged Him to take complete control of her heart and life.

Something wonderful happened during that torrent of words. Danni felt as if God himself stepped into her room, placed His arms around her, and gave her strength to overcome through His power. What started as a prayer of despair turned into a flood of praise for her Savior and Redeemer. That day was one of the best ones Danni ever remembered. She spent the rest of the afternoon humming prayer choruses and focusing on the mercies of the Lord.

Everything went just fine for a few days. But as the weeks passed, Danni began to slip into her old patterns.

Several times she even voiced the negative things she was thinking and allowed her awful attitudes to taint her home's atmosphere. Danni awoke one day to remember that moment of relinquishment months before and the amazing peace that had been hers for a time. Why hadn't she been able to maintain what God had done for her that day?

Encounter God

We will never learn to control our thoughts and tongues and truly be what we need to be to our families unless we first take time to encounter God daily in a radical way. I'm not talking about "Now I lay me down to sleep" or "God, bless this, bless that, bless me." I'm talking about getting on our faces before God, flinging open our hearts to Him, and saying, "Cut me, mold me, do with me as You will. I'm Yours. Totally Yours. A woman after Your heart. Teach me. Show me who You are. Direct me as You will. I will obey." That kind of attitude before God brings a powerful revival in the hearts and minds of women. But true revival is permanent, not something that "wears off." So in order to maintain a spirit of renewal in our homes, this humbling ourselves before God must never be a one-time thing. It must be every day of our lives. Otherwise, we are spiritually off track.

I've never heard a woman say, "I don't ever seem to have time to take a shower. I get up and rush around and think I'll have time to take a shower, but it just doesn't happen. Then lunchtime comes. What a rush! Who has time to shower then? And before I know it, dinnertime arrives. I *have* to eat. I can't take a shower during mealtime. Then there's the rat race of chasing around in the evenings. It seems there's always someone coming over, or we have to go somewhere. Then I flop into bed at night, and before falling to sleep, I realize my shower never happened that day. The next day, the same thing happens all over again. I've finally given up! Showers just weren't meant for me."

Most women wouldn't miss their daily shower, yet many

never take a *spiritual* "shower." This makes a difference in the spiritual aroma of your home, but God has provided a remedy: "Do not conform any longer to the pattern of this world, but be transformed by the renewing of your mind. Then you will be able to test and approve what God's will is— His good, pleasing and perfect will" (Rom. 12:2).

The key word in this verse is *renewing*. It's a present participle verb form that means "ongoing." This renewing must happen every day of our lives if we're to create an aroma of Christ in our homes. In 2 Corinthians Paul states, "But thanks be to God, who always leads us in triumphal procession in Christ and through us spreads everywhere the fragrance of the knowledge of him. For we are to God the aroma of Christ among those who are being saved and those who are perishing" (2:14-15).

If our goal is to be "worth far more than rubies" to our families, then we as Christian women must yearn to have God spread "the fragrance of the knowledge of him" throughout our homes and empower us to be "the aroma of Christ" to our husbands and children. This will occur only when a woman is willing to *habitually* get on her face before Him and touch His heart. As a godly wife, this yearning for the Lord should be our first and most important activity. Everything else in a woman's life hinges on this—peace, integrity, attitude, the atmosphere of the home. Yet often this is the primary area of disobedience in our lives.

The only thing more tragic than a non-Christian saying no to God is when a Christian starts saying no to God. Often we say a resounding yes to Christ at the time of salvation. Everything is great for a while. Then God begins to ask us to abandon ourselves to Him, to seek Him every day of our lives, to allow Him to begin to mold us. And we say no. This inevitably leads to other areas of disobedience in our lives: the attitudes, the criticizing, the complaining, the lack of family prayer time.

God has not called us to live a life of spiritual defeat. He has called us to a victorious, spiritual existence! He has called us to a life that's in tune with Him so that we may feel His power in our homes in an unmistakable way. But that level of power will never happen in a home without a wife who is willing to daily abandon her *all* to the Lord. Along with the renewing of our minds, we must seek God with our whole hearts: "How can a [wife and mother] keep [her] way pure? By living according to your word. I seek you *with all my heart;* do not let me stray from your commands. I have hidden your word in my heart that I might not sin against you" (Ps. 119:9-11, emphasis added).

Are you seeking God with your whole heart? Is worship a general attitude with you every day of your life, or is it just a feigned aura you project at church? Does the atmosphere of your home encourage worship because of your own powerful prayer life?

▷ Danni's Story

These very questions began to haunt Danni. In response to these musings, she desperately tried to start a regular time of prayer and Bible reading. But no matter how hard she tried, she just didn't seem to have what it took to keep a regular appointment with God. She thought that a prayer time would "count" only if she got up an hour before the kids did. But when the alarm clock went off, she found herself groaning and rolling over to snatch a few more minutes of sleep. Then she rushed through her day until evening, when she was too tired to do anything but flop into bed. She found herself having an occasional prayer time, but she never felt as if she really touched God.

After a couple of months of this, Danni found herself in a cycle of failure, guilt, and mental accusations. Even though she and Brice prayed together several times during the week and she continued to initiate family prayer, Danni still struggled with a time when she could have a personal encounter with God. No matter how hard she tried, she just didn't seem to be able to succeed.

At long last, out of sheer desperation, Danni begged

God to show her a daily time when she could encounter Him. Amazingly, the prayer worked! Almost every day she would find a time to seek God simply by listening to the Lord's prompting. Soon she realized that this available time had always been in her schedule, but she had focused elsewhere and missed it.

On Worship

Like Danni, I think we sometimes develop several misconceptions about our personal prayer time. We somehow decide that if we don't get up early every morning for our devotional time that our worship doesn't "count." What I've learned in my pursuit of God is that He wants me to seek Him, and if it's at 6 A.M., fine; if it's at noon, fine; if it's at midnight, fine. Just as long as worship happens. In other words, communion with God can occur anytime, anywhere as long as I'm in a setting that's conducive to focusing on God and hearing His voice.

However, being in a car full of people with the radio blaring is not the kind of worship time that will draw us into the depths of God. Sure—we can breathe all kinds of prayers in that car, and God will hear us. But snatching a prayer here and there is not the quality of prayer that will empower us to create a godly atmosphere in our homes. This type of prayer takes solitude and time.

In Ps. 46 David writes, "Be still, and know that I am God" (v. 10). We'll never have a thriving relationship with God until we're willing to *be still* and *be alone* with Him. And we'll never have a thriving relationship with God by giving Him only a minute or two of our day. How strong would your relationship be with your spouse if the two of you saw each other only one or two minutes a day? And how clean would you be if you spent only one minute a day taking care of personal hygiene? We've been called to a *relationship* with Jesus Christ. No relationship with our Savior happens unless we spend high-quality time and a *good quantity* of time with Him.

*God wants us dining on the honey of his presence, but
we're often lost in the woods, eating tree bark.* Whether we
get our spiritual nourishment at the same time every day
or at differing times, the important thing is that communion with God happens. If your schedule is very predict-
able, then you'll have a better chance of worshiping at the
same time every day. This is great! Furthermore, it's even
greater if your encounter with God can be at the beginning
of your day. In all honesty, I strive for this. There's a lot of
power in starting each day with prayer. Jesus himself
prayed early in the day: "Very early in the morning, while it
was still dark, Jesus got up, left the house and went off to
a solitary place, where he prayed" (Mark 1:35). Furthermore, Lam. 3 says, "Because of the LORD's great love we
are not consumed, for his compassions never fail. They are
new every morning; great is your faithfulness. I say to myself, 'The LORD is my portion; therefore I will *wait for* him.'
The LORD is good to those whose hope is in him, to the one
who seeks him; it is good to *wait quietly* for the salvation
of the LORD" (vv. 22-26, emphasis added).

Even though I strive to wait quietly for the Lord in the
morning, there are some days when, for whatever reason,
that does not happen (most likely for me it's sleep depriva-
tion, because I have two preschoolers). In cases such as
this, you'll find that the prayer Danni prayed asking God to
show her when to worship will be a must if you're going to
have a regular spiritual "bath." If God shows you the best
time is your lunch hour, then so let it be. During the last
few days I have sought God at 6 P.M., 3 A.M., 5 A.M., 12 P.M.,
and 8 P.M. And God's sweet presence filled me every time,
especially the 8 P.M. slot, when He blew my socks off. This
occurred after a trip to the grocery store, car loaded with
groceries, sitting in my driveway, listening to worship music, snatching time alone with the lover of my soul.

Truly, a powerful time alone with God can occur at
any time, in any situation that's conducive to solitude. (But
before you start thinking I'm superspiritual, I must confess

that this morning at 3:00 I felt I should get up and worship the Lord. I didn't. I rolled over like a big old lazy bear and eventually went back to sleep. After I got up this morning, I was able to run to the Cross. But it was on my schedule, not God's. I know I must have missed an immense blessing in the morning's wee hours. I pray that God will give me strength to *always* get up when He calls.)

However, when you begin to ask God daily to show you when you can worship, you'll find that you start embracing most every opportunity to be alone with Him. And sometimes those opportunities come more than once a day. Jesus himself "often withdrew to lonely places and prayed" (Luke 5:16). Also, in the Old Testament Daniel set aside prayer time three times a day (see Dan. 6:10).

Your reaction to this might very well be something like "Yes, but that was the good old days when people had *time*. Do you understand how busy our days are now in the 21st century? Our schedules are tighter and much more fast-paced. People just don't have the time they had in the Bible or even a hundred years ago."

Not true! Since Adam and Eve sinned in the garden, humanity has been consumed with the task of somehow trying to maintain a livelihood, whether carving a living from the land in 1800 or working in a high-tech career in 2000. Think about what it must have been like to live on the frontier. There were no washing machines; clothes were hand-washed with homemade soap. There were no electric ovens or microwaves; food was cooked in a wood-burning stove or over an open fire, and often Mom even helped *cut* the wood. No Wal-Mart or shopping mall. Most wives hand-sewed clothing for the whole family and gave birth to one child each year until they died during labor or they were biologically unable to conceive. I'm sure those women had all sorts of "time" to worship God—right in the middle of chasing after their children, ages newborn, one, two, three, four, five, *and* six, two of which were in hand-washed cloth diapers. Sure, life was slower-paced one or two hundred years ago—because everything took 20 times longer to do!

As in the "good old days," the issue now isn't *time.*
The issue is *priority.* If our ancestors worshiped God more
and had deeper relationships with Him, it's because they
set Him as the top priority in their lives. The God of 500
B.C., A.D. 1000, A.D. 1800, or A.D. 2000 has not changed.
He still wants to develop a "blow your socks off" relationship with us, just as He did with many of our ancestors.

The bottom line is that if we aren't worshiping Him at
home, it's because we really don't make time in our lives.
And that's always been the limiting factor, regardless of the
century. This line is from a song written in the 19th century: "Take time to be holy. The world rushes on."[1]

No matter what the date on the calendar, carving out a
living, taking care of children, and running a household is a
time-consuming business. The question is—am I willing to
put God as the number-one priority in my heart and mind?

A friend of mine in South Carolina, Debbie, has settled
this question once and for all. Now in their 50s, Debbie and
her husband, William, have adopted approximately 25
children, many of whom are handicapped, most of whom
still live with them. Their house teems every day with children—newborns, high schoolers, and kids every age in between. Yet Debbie makes no excuses about her prayer life.
She is determined to meet with her Creator on a regular
basis. And when you enter that home, you know Debbie
has been on her knees, because God's presence glows on
her face and hovers over her home like a cloud of love.
Debbie is a prime example of a woman who represents the
Church to her family. She humbly says, "I'm not Wonder
Woman, but I serve a Wonder God who can do anything!"

When we make God the number-one priority in our
lives, we will *search* for time to sit and gaze upon His holiness, because we desperately want to be like Him. We *always* make time for other priorities in life, such as taking a
shower, putting on makeup, fixing our hair, eating, sleep-
ing, and earning money. If we really desire to impact our
homes and create a godly atmosphere within them, then

we'll take the time to seek God. When you begin to get a taste of the positive, empowering presence of God in your life and home, you'll find the first thing that pops into your mind when you snatch a moment alone is "Finally—I can be with the Lord now!"

The following tips will expedite your journey to that point:

1. **Ask God for help.** If you don't currently have a vital time with God of 30 minutes to an hour a day, pray that God will provide an opportunity for you to worship daily. Sometimes for me, that's getting up early. Sometimes, it's staying up late. Sometimes it's getting up at 1 A.M. and sitting at the feet of the Lover of my soul until 2 A.M. Sometimes it means using some of my office hours—the time that I've paid a baby-sitter to watch my two preschool children so I can write. Worship is more important to God than serving Him. Therefore, I often worship first and then write.

We have a tendency to say, "Lord, I'll do whatever You want me to do" when God calls us to be in His presence.

If we're petitioning God to help us in this area, He'll answer our request in amazing ways. For instance, one of the most powerful worship times I've ever experienced occurred while I was driving my car at night with a worship cassette playing. Pray that God will come near every day and tug you into His presence.

2. **Buy worship music.** Currently I'm using a collection of worship tapes. Some are choruses; some are solo instrumentals. God-centered music truly empowers us to focus on the Lord. While I read my Bible, I enjoy hearing a faint background of solo piano music. I also enjoy it while I pray. During prayer I enjoy prayer choruses, because I can sing the lyrics to the One I'm in awe of. You might be the kind of person whom music distracts while you're reading. That's fine and quite normal for some. If you don't want to play music during your devotional time, then don't ignore the power in using worship music throughout the day. Even if you aren't in a "planned" worship session, godly music

turns your heart and focus to the One who created you. If you do choose to use music during your worship time, either after or before reading the Word and bringing requests to God, allow the music to wash over you, and listen for God's voice in your soul. In reality, this is what prayer is all about: listening to God and allowing *Him* to minister to *us*.

3. Focus your thoughts on God, and allow Him to guide and direct you. Prayer is more about listening to God than stating my list of requests. We *should* bring our list of requests to Him—"Do not be anxious about anything, but in everything, by prayer and petition, with thanksgiving, present your requests to God" (Phil. 4:6). But just as important is sitting at Jesus' feet, absorbing His presence, meditating on Him. When you start doing this, you'll find that scriptures will come to you as special messages He wants to place in your heart. You'll also begin to hear God's voice through the thoughts that come to you. But remember: God never instructs us or speaks to us in terms that don't align themselves with the Bible. Nonetheless, meditating on Him renews our minds. This is our spiritual "bath."

4. Organize your prayer requests. My friend Cindy educated me in this important step. Using her example, I have a list that I use quite often. Almost every day I pray for a family member, a friend, a missionary, an unsaved person, and a group (such as the neighborhood, the United States, or my professional associates). Every day the specific names are different for each category. I suggest you use such a list. Furthermore, keep a running list of daily requests. Put your husband and children at the top. Carry it in your purse. You can buy pocket-sized notebooks that have snap flaps, which are perfect for this, or you can now buy purses that have organizers built into them. So when a friend mentions a prayer request or shares a problem, you can take out your daily prayer list and jot it down. Then during your prayer time you won't forget those you're supposed to pray for. If none of these methods appeals to you, then do what works best for you.

5. Develop a plan in reading the Word. In my *Women's Devotional Bible,* if I read eight pages a day, I can read through the entire Bible in six months. Four pages a day will get me through the Bible in one year. Also realize that Bible reading and Bible study are different. Both are important. I recommend Bible studies by Aletha Hinthorn (published by Beacon Hill Press of Kansas City) or Kay Arthur or even the well-known study called *Experiencing God.* Whatever your plan is, develop one and stick to it.

6. Meditate on the Word. Choose a scripture to think on during the day. For the last several days, I've been focusing on "Be still, and know that I am God" (Ps. 46:10). A very practical method to incorporate meditation in your life is to buy the Daily Bread scriptures printed on narrow cards that come in a plastic container shaped like a loaf of bread. Regularly tape one of these Bible verses onto your bathroom mirror or onto your car's dashboard. Every time you go to the rest room or get into your car, your verse will be waiting on you. Meditating on scripture unleashes God's power in your thought life and develops self-control in your thoughts as well as other areas of life.

In Ps. 119 David writes, "I have hidden your word in my heart that I might not sin against you" (v. 11). Understand that choosing a scripture that addresses a particular weak point in your life will bring victory where defeat once reigned. Right now I'm praying that God will strengthen me in scripture meditation.

7. Realize failures. There will be days when you think, "I really need to worship God," and for whatever reason, you don't. There are times when I do exactly that. But just because you skip devotions for a day or two doesn't mean God is somehow mad at you and won't honor your desire to be alone with Him the next time you kneel at His feet. Ideally, you should strive to be alone with God every day, and I try really hard to accomplish this goal. But on the days I don't, I'm tempted to fall into a full-blown guilt trip. I believe this is Satan's trap to keep us from worshiping at all. Just keep trying. If you go a few days without a shower, everyone will be glad when you take one. Similarly, going a few days without being with the Lord will soon become obvious to your whole family. Both they and God will be glad when you pick up where you left off.

8. Pray that God will give you a prayer partner. This is important, because you can be accountable to each other and share areas of struggle. Even though my husband and I are prayer partners and we share our spiritual journey with each other, I also enjoy having prayer partners who are female and close to my own age. There have been seasons when my prayer partner(s) and I have regularly met together for prayer and sharing. Then there are seasons when we might not meet together but simply share requests and pray for each other while keeping each other accountable. There's an enormous amount of comfort in having a confidential prayer partner(s) with whom you can safely share.

Let us fix our eyes on Jesus, the author and perfecter of our faith, who for the joy set before him endured the cross, scorning its shame, and sat down at the right hand of the throne of God. Consider him who endured such opposition from sinful men, so that you will not grow weary and lose heart. In your struggle against sin, you have not yet resisted to the point of shedding your blood.

—Heb. 12:2-4

▷ Danni's Story

After Danni began regularly worshiping God at home, she noticed some amazing changes in her life. The atmosphere in her home and family seemed much calmer, more peaceful, and full of God's presence. While her junior high children by no means sprouted wings and halos, they were putting up fewer and fewer emotional barriers between themselves and their mom. Since Danni had made her husband top priority in everyday prayer, their relationship began to blossom in amazing ways, and she watched with wonder as Brice began to grow by leaps and bounds spiritually—simply because she had stopped accusing and started praying. Mortified, Danni realized that her past negative influence had actually hindered Brice's spiritual growth.

Danni herself began to feel God's presence in a new and powerful way. Everywhere she turned she saw the Lord at work. She experienced miraculous answers to prayer. She had a deeper appreciation for the handiwork of God—virtually every tree, field, and star. She marveled at the miracle of birth and at the gifts of her own children.

Every church service Danni attended seemed full of God's presence. This astounded her. She had long ago stopped "getting anything" out of church. The services had seemed dry and lifeless. Now Danni realized it was because she had been spiritually dry, lifeless, and unpleasant. She began to see that what happens at home with God spills over into what happens at church. In the past, she had expected church to "carry her" through the week rather than to reinforce what was already happening at home with her own personal relationship with God.

Furthermore, Danni felt a new and overwhelming sense of love for every person she encountered, especially her own family. She loved her husband more than ever. She appreciated her children and began to treasure the time she had with them rather than resenting their "intrusion" upon her "space." There had been a few people at church whom she had long ago started avoiding because she "didn't like them." But Danni somehow was able to look past what she perceived as their abrasiveness and see them the way God sees them. She realized that her thriving relationship with God sweetened every association.

After a few weeks of being on a spiritual high, Danni began to feel uncomfortable about some things that God started bringing to her mind—negative behavior that she had not made restitution for, bad attitudes that she had not confessed, people she had not forgiven. At first she panicked and suppressed the convicting thoughts that suggested she should begin to ask family members and friends to forgive her for specific sins.

Was this of God? Surely God wouldn't ask her to make amends to people when she had not been the one totally in the wrong. But the thoughts continued to nag at her and seemed to be worse during her prayer time. At long last, Danni acknowledged that God himself was asking her to begin making restitution, and she realized with dread that obeying Him was probably going to cost her every scrap of pride she had ever possessed.

> *A wife of noble character who can find?*
> *She is worth far more than rubies. . . .*
> *Charm is deceptive, and beauty is fleeting;*
> *but a woman who fears the LORD is*
> *to be praised. Give her the reward*
> *she has earned, and let her works*
> *bring her praise at the city gate.*

                    —Prov. 31:10, 30-31

Ruby "Am I's"

1. Am I spreading unpleasantness throughout my household?
     Evidence that you are: You are not seriously seeking God on a regular basis.

2. Am I God-focused rather than self-focused?
     Evidence that you are: You're more interested in what

God thinks of you rather than what you think of a certain person or situation.

3. Am I saying no to God in any area of my life?

   Evidence that you are: When you start thinking of developing a regular time of Bible reading and earnest, soul-searching prayer, the first thing that pops into your head is, "If I start that, then I know God will require me to obey in this particular area, and I don't want to."

4. Am I finding excuses for not making a dynamic and powerful prayer life a top priority?

   Evidence that you are: You often say things like "Back in the good old days, people just had more time to pursue God."

5. Am I hindering my husband's spiritual growth?

   Evidence that you are: Instead of earnestly praying for him, you often mentally "take inventory" of him and tally all the areas you see that need growth.

Ruby "Ifs"

1. If you don't have a powerful prayer life:

- Buy worship music.

- Focus your thoughts on God. He'll guide you.

- Organize your prayer requests.

- Develop a plan for reading the Word.

2. If you try to pray and don't feel His presence:

- Start by reading Scripture. Often the Word of God opens our hearts to His presence.

- Ask God to direct you in your prayers.

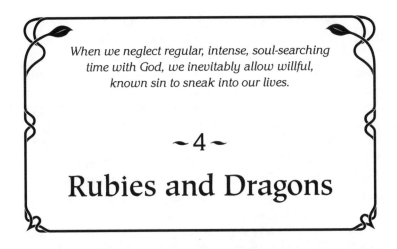

*When we neglect regular, intense, soul-searching
time with God, we inevitably allow willful,
known sin to sneak into our lives.*

~ 4 ~

Rubies and Dragons

▷ **Danni's Story**

Danni began doing to herself what she had once done
to Brice. She began "taking inventory." At long last she
thought, "Forget Brice and his faults. I've got too much
wrong with me to keep worrying about him." She left Brice
at the top of her daily prayer list and told God that his spiritual growth was between him and the Lord. This freed her
to get a clear, although sickening, view of herself. Danni's
self-inventory showed that during all those years she had
not been on her face before God in her spirit, she had let
"little" sins sneak into her life and made excuses for them
as "just the way I am."

Those sins had started out about the size of scorpions.
But as she fed them with a steady diet of excuses and an
ample supply of other unpleasant things they grew to the
size of crocodiles. Before she knew it, those sins matured
into nothing short of dragons, chained to her neck. Their
munching and crunching and stomping and howling had
affected her every relationship. Everywhere she went, she
had pulled those fiery beasts with her. For years, they had
sucked every ounce of a worshipful spirit from her home
and filled it with their foul breath.

As her inventory continued, Danni remembered all those years she failed to earnestly seek God and had settled into bed with a "daily prayer," ready on her lips: *Dear Lord, thank You for this day. Help me to do better. Amen.* In reality, she had been in direct disobedience to God because she was not earnestly seeking Him even though she pretended that everything was OK.

Danni soon realized that the dragons were the sins that God was asking her to confess, repent of, and make restitution for. At first she tried to just do half of what God was asking. After all, going to people she had wronged, confessing her sin, and asking for forgiveness was going to be humiliating, to say the least. So she asked God to forgive her, and she truly repented. But Danni soon realized that she had carried out only half of His instructions, which still amounted to disobedience.

Every time she read the Bible, up popped annoying verses such as, "He who conceals his sins does not prosper, but whoever confesses and renounces them finds mercy" (Prov. 28:13). "Confess your sins to each other and pray for each other so that you may be healed. The prayer of a righteous man is powerful and effective" (James 5:16). Stumbling over these verses, Danni realized that she had confessed her sins to no one against whom she had sinned. She also realized that as long as she had not pursued righteousness, her prayers had been neither powerful nor effective.

Another passage began to haunt her—words from Jesus: "If you hold to my teaching, you are really my disciples. Then you will know the truth, and the truth will set you free. . . . I tell you the truth, everyone who sins is a slave to sin" (John 8:31-32, 34). A light went on in Danni's heart. She realized that she had been a slave to her dragons. She hadn't been dragging them around. *They* did the pushing, shoving, jerking, and inciting her to behave in an un-Christlike, selfish manner. Then came the big blow: "Whatever is hidden is meant to be disclosed, and whatev-

er is concealed is meant to be brought out into the open"
(Mark 4:22).

At that point, Danni saw there were no other choices.
The only door open was marked "Make restitution." She
knew in the deepest cavity of her soul that those stacked-
up sins had affected not only her relationship with God but
also her relationship with almost every friend and relative.
The place God showed Danni to start was in her own
home. One night during family prayer time, through a torrent of tears, she confessed to her family that she had allowed her sins of prayerlessness, criticism, complaining,
and a bad attitude to destroy the godly atmosphere in their
home. She further told them that she had asked God to
forgive her and begged them to also forgive her.

The result was beautiful. Everybody in the family embraced her. No eyes were dry that night. A new spirit of ca-
maraderie blanketed the home. A new glint of respect
brightened the eyes of Brice and her children. Furthermore,
the next time the family prayed together, Danni found that
her own confession freed the rest of her family to confess
their shortcomings and sins. The change brought a new
power to their family, a new sense of "Let's lift one another
up in prayer as we strive to be Christlike together."

Thus, Danni began the difficult journey of being completely truthful with everyone around her, confessing her
sins, and enjoying freedom from those horrid dragons. The
path took her to members of her extended family, to people she had worked with, to friends, to neighbors. Simply
put, every time God brought a negative situation to her
mind and showed her where she had sinned, she confessed, repented, and made restitution. Sometimes restor-
ing relationships cost her every scrap of dignity she
thought she possessed. But she did it anyway. For the
most part, those to whom she confessed were gracious
and forgiving. Danni's relationship with them was strength-
ened beyond her expectation. However, there were times
the person she approached condemned and pointed a

judgmental finger at her. In those situations, Danni remained amazingly calm, showed love to the person, and
walked away with God's blessing. For she was now inter-
ested in pleasing God more than she was intent on defend-
ing herself.

Soon Danni was astounded to see the impact of an
honest and contrite spirit. She was able to use her own failures as a way to point out God's grace and witness to
those who might not otherwise know personal testimonies
to His power. Furthermore, she realized God used the confession of her sins to bring about something powerful and
good in her own life as well as the lives of those she
touched. For once, Danni was a living example of an
amazing and freeing biblical principle.

Sin

I must be honest. While Danni isn't always me in this
book, in this chapter she is indeed mostly me. Because I
started panting for God "as the deer pants for streams of
water" (Ps. 42:1), God dramatically required that I begin to
make amends in relationships in which I had not been
Christlike. You might say, "Yeah, but look at all you've
been through in life. You aren't perfect. Anybody would
have developed some attitude problems and done some
things wrong." Of course. And I believe that there were
times when God's grace covered me until I was mentally,
spiritually, and emotionally healed enough to see my sin.
Nonetheless, that does not excuse my sin, and it does not
excuse my lack of restitution.

We have a tendency to excuse sin based on circumstances. Circumstances are no excuse for sin or for a lack
of Christlikeness. It's never acceptable for me to respond
to someone's sin in a disobedient way. In other words, if
someone attacks me verbally, returning the attack only results in wrong on top of wrong, even if the initial attack
was unfounded.

If there have been times in your life such as this, a

radical encounter with Jesus Christ always results in experiencing what the woman at the well experienced: "Come, see a man who told me everything I ever did" (John 4:29). If we get serious with Jesus Christ, He *will* tell us everything we have ever done. At that point, we have a choice. We can either drink His living water, embrace His forgiveness, and make restitution as He leads, or we can say no. A no inevitably leads to the sin of lost communication, because we cannot pray without Jesus Christ once again bringing to mind that item He has asked us to make right. His conviction makes us miserable. In order to avoid misery, we avoid prayer. This only leads to more sin.

When we neglect regular, soul-searching time with God, we inevitably allow willful, known sin to sneak into our lives. Often we try to cover the sin with excuses or deny it altogether. I call this "the Adam-and-Eve thing." In Gen. 3 after Adam and Eve sinned, they hid from God, as if He couldn't find them or didn't see through their plot to hide. We often do the same thing. We might have a myriad of "dragons" chained to our necks. In an attempt to hide their presence, we put a dish towel over each of them and say, "What sin, God? What are You talking about?" When we finally admit the sin, often the tendency arises to pass the blame to someone else, as when Adam accused Eve and she faulted the serpent. We say something like, "Sure, I was hateful and said some things I shouldn't have, Lord. But she started it! And she was far worse than I was!" We pretend someone else's sin justifies our own.

There's a paradox here: When comparing myself with others, there's always someone who's "worse" than I am, and I'll naturally come out looking good. But I'm not. The reason for the false assumption: a wrong standard. I must forever compare myself to *Jesus Christ.* This puts the picture of me in its proper perspective. According to Oswald Chambers, "Many of us have a mental picture of what a Christian should be, and looking at this [lack of] image in other Christians' lives becomes a hindrance to our focusing

on God"[1] and allowing the Lord to reveal our own failings
to us.

When we use the wrong example long enough, we
soon forget to "be the Church" to our families, to be a vehicle through which God's Spirit can permeate every corner
of our homes. Every night we might go to sleep as Danni
(and I) did with "Lord, bless my home, and help me to do
better." But in reality we need to confess, repent, and make
restitution for the sins we're in denial about.

Remember—it's one thing for me to fail and therefore
ask God and my neighbor to forgive me. It's another thing
altogether for me to live a *lifestyle* of sin—in either attitudes or actions. That is not and never has been God's
plan. Paul writes, "Count yourselves dead to sin but alive
to God in Christ Jesus. Therefore do not let sin reign in
your mortal body so that you obey its evil desires. Do not
offer the parts of your body to sin, as instruments of
wickedness, but rather offer yourselves to God, as those
who have been brought from death to life; and offer the
parts of your body to him as instruments of righteousness"
(Rom. 6:11-13). David expresses this in Ps. 119:133 with
"Direct my footsteps according to your word; let no sin rule
over me."

Any woman living a lifestyle of sin and harboring un-
Christlike attitudes and actions will find her home filled
with stinky "dragon" breath, not the presence of God. If a
woman has not been seeking God with her whole heart,
once she starts, God will continually bring these sins to
mind and ask her not only to confess and repent but also
to make amends.

Change occurs only when a woman gets totally serious with God. No games—just you and God, and you saying, "Do with me what You will. Melt me. Mold me. I'm
Yours." If you've never sought God on this level, you had
better be ready for pain. The process takes guts. This is
not easy stuff. It's tough—really tough. There were times
during my two-year season of restitution and purging that I

spiritually ached to my toenails. But complete abandonment and obedience is a must if we want our lives to be a
godly influence on our family and our world.

The Cycle of Confession

Be convinced—God is faithful. He never asks us to do
anything that isn't for our good and that will not bring
about spiritual strength, complete with His blessings. When
you truly seek God in your life, you'll notice a cycle of
blessing, obedience, and purging. Initially God will bless
your desire to seek Him. Then He will ask your obedience
in a specific area. This brings purging in that area of disobedience. Your obedience and willingness to allow God to
purge you will bring His renewed blessing. Then you'll start
all over. Peter writes, "Now that you have *purified* yourselves by *obeying the truth* so that you have sincere love
for your brothers, love one another deeply, from the heart"
(1 Pet. 1:22, emphasis added).

When I started coming to God and saying, "Here I
am—do with me what You will," He blessed that in an
amazing way. Then He began to require my obedience.
Many times I struggled, rationalized, tried to find any
means of escape, but at long last I always obeyed. This re-
sulted in God purging that area of my life. Sometimes that
purging hurt deeply. But after each obedient act, after each
purging, God increased the blessing.

Once again, this is where so many Christians begin to
say no. They don't want this kind of radical obedience because it might cost their pride or even their social standing.
The area of radical obedience that hurts the deepest and
humbles us the greatest is making restitution, the process
of confessing our sins and allowing God to use that to re-
store relationships. Truly, Peter knew what he was talking
about in the above verse when he said, "Now that you
have purified yourselves by obeying the truth so that you
have sincere love for your brothers, love one another
deeply, from the heart." Clearly, obedience and purification

go hand in hand, and that results in "sincere love for your brothers" and sisters and friends and husband and children and business associates.

Sin can never be an isolated incident between God and me. If I sin, others are affected. But most important my whole family is affected, because even if the sin isn't directly against them, it inhibits my ability to minister to them as I should. When that happens, I must confess, repent, and make amends with the party I have sinned against. This frees me from the "dragons" that will inevitably hinder the spirit of my home. Never doubt that God is faithful to take what we've done wrong and turn it into a positive testimony of His redeeming grace if we'll simply obey Him. And as my friend D. L. Stewart says, "As long as I make God look good, I don't have to worry about whether or not *I* look good."

Two True Stories

My friend Ruth experienced God's faithfulness in turning her 20-year-old sin into a miraculous testimony and proof of God's divine guidance. When Ruth was in junior high school, she was the concession stand manager at her Christian school. Satan tempted her to steal money from the concession stand, and she yielded to his voice. For 20 years she never thought about that sin.

Then—the ominous *then*—Ruth started seriously seeking God *with her whole heart.* And God began to bring that sin to her mind and impress upon her that she needed to make restitution to the school. Ruth did what I always tend to do—she began to rationalize. According to Oswald Chambers, "We put our common sense on the throne and then attach God's name to it. We *do* lean to our own understanding, instead of trusting [the voice of] God with all our hearts."[2] Ruth's rationalization went something like this: "But it's been 20 years since I stole that money! I have no idea how much I stole, so there's no way I can repay it. The whole staff, including the principal, has probably changed since then. Nobody even knew I took the money. Why would God ask me to confess that sin?" So she pushed the issue down in the recesses of her soul and tried to ignore it.

Every time she went to prayer, however, that sin was before her. She couldn't pray, and she had stopped growing spiritually. At last she acknowledged with sickening reality that she was going to have to make restitution or be in direct disobedience to God.

At this point, many people simply say no, go on with their lives, show up in church, smile, and, like Samson, never realize that God's power has left them (Judg. 16:20). In reality, they have just given birth to another "scorpion" that will soon grow into a "dragon" of disobedience, which will be a close companion to the original sin that spawned it.

But Ruth did not fall into this trap. Instead, she gritted her teeth, prayed like crazy, and wrote her letter of confession and restitution to the parent-sponsored booster club. Along with the letter, she knew she needed to send money to replace what she took. However, she couldn't remember exactly how much she had stolen. After much prayer, God impressed her to send $80. So she mailed the letter with an $80 check.

Several weeks went by, and Ruth began to wonder if she would ever hear any response to the letter that cost her every scrap of pride she ever possessed. At long last she received a letter from the booster club president. He was astounded and blessed that she had possessed the character to confess such a sin. But he went on to relate an equally astounding story.

The school had a girls' softball team. A young woman on the team needed a glove, and her family simply didn't have the money to buy one. So the school coach purchased the glove with his own money. As a Christian, he prayerfully bought the glove on faith. Because he didn't have the extra money, he trusted God to replace the funds. Then they received Ruth's check for $80. *The glove* had cost $80!

God took Ruth's obedience and turned it into something beautiful, into an amazing witness of His power and love for each of us. But if Ruth had not obeyed Him, she and her family would have been left with a dragon amongst them. Her godly influence would have been limited by her own disobedience.

A dear friend of mine recently volunteered to be one of the staff members in charge of a Christian women's retreat. Her duty was to assign seating. She stayed up until 2 and 3 A.M. the week before, working through this highly difficult task. This was in the middle of her duties as a pastor's wife and her casework as an international adoption facilitator.

The retreat took place on a Friday night and Saturday. By the time it ended, she was ready to pull out her hair. This is basically the story she related to me:

> You wouldn't believe the misery I've been dealt by the women at this retreat. They want to sit exactly where they want to sit, and if they don't get their way, they're throwing fits right in front of me. Over and over again I've been the victim of temper tantrums because, of all things, *seating!*

> One woman even said, "Fine! If I can't sit where I want to sit, then I'll just not eat my meal!"

> I smiled and said, "That's all right. But your choice doesn't in any way affect me. You're just hurting yourself."

> I just can't believe this, Debra! These are supposed to be Christian women!

As time rolled on, to my knowledge none of those women apologized to my friend, who had *sacrificially* given of her time and energy to try to make the women's retreat a positive experience. And guess what—those women, whoever they are, by this point have two new dragons chained to their necks to add to the collection of dragons with which they came to that retreat: the dragon of behaving in an un-Christlike manner and the dragon of disobedience in not making amends.

To Restitute or Not to Restitute

At this point, God might be bringing instances to your mind in which you should have made restitution but didn't. Don't feel alone! The lost son in Luke 15:11-32 is a prime example of someone who knew he had to make restitution. He greatly sinned against his father when he *told* the father to give him his inheritance. This was a highly rebellious and rare request. Legally, the father could have had the son stoned. But he didn't. Instead, he gave the son his money and watched him walk out of his life. The son lived high until he got to a point where it was just God and him . . . and, of course, the pigs. That's when "he came to his senses" (v. 17).

This story illustrates exactly what we do. We often commit a sin against God and someone and go on our "merry way" until we have a moment when it's just God and ourselves. That's when God brings us to our senses, as He did the son, and compels us to confess, repent, and make restitution. If we're to maintain a godly atmosphere in our homes, we must go back where our sin was commit- ted and declare, "'I have sinned against heaven and against you' [Luke 15:21]. I'm sorry. Please forgive me."

It's important to know that every unrepented sin will affect the atmosphere of the home. So whether or not the sin was against your family members, even if it was a se- cret, rebellious musing of your heart, that sin will affect re- lationships in your home. You cannot tow a dragon with you everywhere you go without consequences to the at- mosphere of your home. Known, willful sin does affect all our relationships. Therefore, every sin must be confessed to God and repented of. Repentance means that, with God as my helper, I will do everything in my power not to com- mit that sin again.

But does every sin require restitution with my neigh- bor? No. In some instances it might be best not to confess the sin to the involved party.

For example, let's say I have a terrible, critical attitude

toward a friend. I struggle with that attitude and pray for God's power and deliverance from it. I at last ask His forgiveness and repent of my sin. Meanwhile, the person I was having the bad attitude about, who lives three states away, has no idea that I was fuming about her. Therefore, it's not very wise for me to call her up, tell her about my anger, and ask her forgiveness. In doing this, I would wound this person who otherwise would never have been wounded. Christ came to heal and reconcile. Likewise, our restitution should reflect His mission.

If you're struggling with whether or not a particular situation requires restitution, contemplate the following questions:

1. Is the concerned party aware of my sin against him or her? If so, then restitution is always a must unless approaching the concerned party will risk your life or involve threat of physical danger.

2. Will the restitution bring healing? Let's pretend that my attitude toward the friend three states away was a way of life for me and that this person knew I felt negatively toward her. It will indeed bring healing if I make restitution. However, I still do not need to detail every negative thought I ever had about her. This will only bring more wounds. God is in the business of healing relationships, just as He did with the lost son in Luke. Therefore, your restitution should be targeted for healing. There was an instance in my own season of restitution when I felt God impressing me to apologize, and I argued that the concerned party didn't even know I had struggled with an attitude toward her. But God was persistent. I finally made restitution and discovered that the concerned person indeed *did* know I held an un-Christlike attitude toward her. Make sure you listen to God's prompting. Sometimes our body language and facial expressions will communicate our heart even when our words do not.

3. Will it represent Christ well? If your restitution is only an obligatory act based on feelings of guilt, and there has been no repentance, then it will not represent Christ well. For instance, let's say I do lambaste my friend three states away. But after a while, I start feeling bad about the whole thing, so I go to her and apologize. Meanwhile, she starts lambasting *me* for accosting her in the first place. I return the rage and storm back to my home three states away. This does nothing but cheapen Christ's power and His death on the Cross. Restitution represents Christ well only when I continue to behave in a Christlike manner toward the person in question, even in the face of his or her anger. Restitution is powerful, but only if I have first truly repented. Furthermore, restitution should never be made with a superior attitude or as a means to manipulate the person to say, "I'm sorry," as well. If the person is still pointing a finger at you when you're already humble and contrite before him or her (this has happened to me), then gracefully and prayerfully disengage yourself from the conversation. Later you can respond to that person's negative behavior by doing good to him or her. Only then will you represent Christ well.

4. **Will there be spiritual profit from it?** This can come in the form of my own spiritual profit or that of another. For instance, I once made restitution about something the concerned party did not know I had done. But I was able to use the sin as a witnessing tool to this unsaved person. I said something to the affect that I was a Christian who was undergoing a time of spiritual purging and that I felt that I must confess my wrongdoing and ask for forgiveness. Therefore, God was able to use my confession to point to my Savior as the One who forgives. This confession brought spiritual profit to me because I obeyed God. However, it also brought the potential of spiritual profit to the person I confessed to because it pointed the person to Christ. Remember the example of Ruth's repaying $80. No one knew she had taken the money, even at the time she took it. Yet God required her to make restitution because He had a divine plan that brought glory to Him.

Several years ago a friend called me to apologize for being rude. I was astounded at her apology, because I never recalled her being rude. I remembered the incident she related, but I had not taken her behavior negatively. None-theless, she knew she had been rude. God knew she had been rude. And she thought I knew she had been rude. So she apologized and asked my forgiveness. After I got off the phone with her, my first thoughts were, "That was great of her." Then, I started developing an attitude of my own! This rudeness she confessed was now fresh news to me, and it began to annoy me. For a while I said, "I wish she had never told me." But when I truly forgave her and the annoyance vanished, I began to have respect for the courage it took for her to apologize to me. That respect deepened when God began to require that *I* make restitu-tion to people *I* had wronged. And in reality, I think our friendship is stronger because of her honesty, even though I initially didn't know she had been rude. In short, she set a good spiritual example for me.

5. **Is the conflict with me or with truth?** Suppose someone comes to you and says, "I want your opinion on whether or not I should have an affair." And you tell him or her in a loving, firm way that an affair is a sin and will bring nothing but heartache into his or her life. You further suggest in a nonjudgmental, Christlike manner that this person needs to once and for all get serious with God. Now suppose this person becomes furious with you and storms out of your life. As long as you have remained Christlike and simply stated truth without condemnation, the conflict is not with you—it is with truth. In order to correct the problem, you most likely will have to compromise truth, but that is never God's way. You owe no restitution. However, it's very easy to self-righteously pretend that every conflict is not with you, but with truth, just so you can get out of restitution. Make certain that you don't use this criteria as a means of excus-ing your own negative, un-Christlike behavior.

6. **What does God say?** You may be in torment about something as serious as a long-ago-ended affair success-fully hidden from your mate for 20 years. I have heard dif-fering views on whether or not hidden sins of this nature

should be confessed to the injured, although blissfully ig-
norant, party. Some Christian professionals say yes. Some
Christian authorities such as pastor-author Stan Toler say,
"If the sin is over and under the blood of Jesus, the admis-
sion might be a mistake."[3] Furthermore, I have a Christian
acquaintance who, 25 years after his wife's confession of
an affair, still wishes she had never told him. On the other
hand, if the injured party is suspicious and asks probing
questions, that puts a different angle on the whole situation
and will most likely require confession. If you are uncertain
about *any* particular hidden sin and whether or not it requires restitution, spend a season of intense prayer about
the issue. If you can get peace with God about it, then accept God's forgiveness, forgive yourself, and release it to
Him. If you cannot get peace, carefully seek the advice of
a trained, knowledgeable Christian counselor who will pray
with you, not just advise. Also make certain that your lack
of peace is indeed God's way of asking you to make restitution and is not simply your own inability to forgive yourself. On the other hand, make doubly sure your supposed
peace isn't the product of stuffing your true feelings and ignoring the voice of God.

Purposes of Restitution

God's laws and requirements all have perfectly logical
and valuable reasons behind them. God does not ask us to
abstain from or participate in any particular activity on
some supernatural whim. In other words, if God asks us to
do something, it's because He's a loving Heavenly Father
who wants what is absolutely best for us. Restitution is one
of those things that is for our best.

Jesus stated, "If you are offering your gift at the altar
and there remember that your brother has something
against you, leave your gift there in front of the altar. First go
and be reconciled to your brother; then come and offer your
gift" (Matt. 5:23-24). Align this scripture with Eph. 4:25-27:
"Each of you must put off falsehood and speak truthfully to

his neighbor, for we are all members of one body. 'In your anger do not sin': Do not let the sun go down while you are still angry, and do not give the devil a foothold." These verses outline five valid, logical reasons for restitution:

1. A lack of it affects our time with God. Our time with God will not be the powerful experience it can be if we are not willing to completely come clean with Him and our neighbor.

2. Restitution brings reconciliation and healing. Our relationship with God is both horizontal and vertical. If we truly love God, we'll love our neighbor and do everything in our power to show that love (1 John 4:20).

3. Restitution requires honesty. Notice in Eph. 4:25-26 the close proximity of telling the truth to the issue of anger. Often anger can be disintegrated when we lovingly approach the concerned party and honestly share from the heart.

4. Restitution stops the devil from getting a foothold in our lives. There's a reason Paul wrote, "Do not let the sun go down while you are still angry" (Eph. 4:26). The longer we hold out on making restitution and the longer we harbor anger and resentment, the more authority we give the devil in our lives. Satan is described many times in Revelation as a dragon, specifically in chapter 12. The "dragons" chained around Danni's neck represent the footholds of Satan himself.

5. Restitution develops self-control. God brings forth this important element of the fruit of the Spirit in our lives (see Gal. 5:22) when we radically obey Him. For instance, do you think I will *ever* be rude to anyone again? Forget it! I'll do everything in my power *not* to be rude, because I know that if I'm ill-mannered, God will tap me on the shoulder. Do you think Ruth will *ever* steal another dollar in her life? No way! If God requires you to make restitution, He also teaches you not to repeat the offense. *Restitution is God's way of making us humbly take responsibility for our actions and therefore teaching us, though His power, to control ourselves.*

This is not about earning God's forgiveness. His forgiveness was complete on the Cross. Restitution is an avenue through which God trains and guides us to be like Him. It is also about tapping into a biblical principle that will free us from any footholds Satan might have in our lives, otherwise known as "the dragons." Restitution means to "make every effort to live in peace with all men and to be holy" (Heb. 12:14).

▷ Danni's Story

Because Danni lived in radical obedience to God, making restitution where He required it, she began to see a supernatural power being released in her prayer time. For the first time in her life, God's presence was so real to Danni that she literally craved His touch. She eagerly looked forward to her prayer times. She could hardly wait to get alone with the God who had become the Lover of her soul. Indeed, she felt as if she were addicted to His presence. She began to devour Scripture. She ate, drank, and slept the presence of God. She became God-focused and sensed His love in almost every breath.

As a result, Danni's home was permeated with Almighty God. She felt as if a cloud of love had descended into every corner of her household. For the first time in her life, Danni was learning what it truly meant to be a powerful instrument of God and effectively minister to her family.

A wife of noble character who can find?
She is worth far more than rubies. . . .
She brings . . . good, not harm,
all the days of her life.

—Prov. 31:10, 12

Ruby "Am I's"

1. Am I chained to "dragon sins" that are destroying the godly atmosphere in my home?

Evidence that you are: You have not regularly continued a soul-searching, *intense* prayer life.

2. Am I going to have to make restitution with someone?
   Evidence that you are: While reading this chapter, you repeatedly thought of one or more situations in which you did not behave in a Christlike manner. When you close the book, you might be able to get away from these tormenting thoughts, but when you try to pray, they'll be back.

3. Am I guilty of allowing the sin of pride to stop me from making restitution?
   Evidence that you are: You stiffly have thoughts such as "I refuse to lower myself to that task."

4. Am I trying to rationalize situations in which I have sinned against my family or acquaintances?
   Evidence that you are: You often act out the "Adam and Eve thing," justifying your own sin by highlighting the sins of others or by passing blame. You may say things like "I might not have been exactly Christlike, but look how horrible *she* was. I only responded to her initial sin."

5. Am I living at my full spiritual potential at this given moment?
   Evidence that you are: You have been living in radical obedience to God, making restitution where He requires it and staying on your face before Him in your spirit.

Ruby "Ifs"

If you're contemplating making restitution, allow the following questions to guide you:

- **Is the concerned party aware of my sin against him or her?**

- **Will the restitution bring healing?**

- **Will it represent Christ well?**

- **Will there be spiritual profit from it?**

- **Is the conflict with me or with truth?**

- **What does God say?**

~5~

Rubies and Roses

▷ Danni's Story

When Danni was freed of the dragons, she not only felt God's wonderful power in her home but also found that praise was ready on her lips. Living close to God was such a positive experience that she just naturally exhibited positive thoughts and actions. In the past she had always enjoyed hearing the latest negative tidbit about her acquaintances, but now she found that she tried to steer conversations toward what was right with people rather than what was wrong with them.

Then there was Brice. In the past Danni had seen more of what was wrong with the man than what was right. Shamefully, she recalled the times she had criticized him in front of her children. Now she desperately desired to build him up, praise him, encourage him, and make him feel that he was important to her and to God.

Brice responded to her praise in an amazing way. He became more complimentary of Danni, and their marriage began to blossom in new and astounding directions. After almost 20 years of marriage, the two of them seemed to be truly best friends and soul mates instead of two individuals living in the same home but sharing little. As a result of the new dimension in their relationship and Danni's continual praise of her husband, her children began to respect Brice on a new level. Danni watched in amazement as they began to reflect her own treatment of Brice.

Danni's teenagers also began putting up fewer and fewer barriers between themselves and their mom. They seemed to glow when Danni praised them. She even praised their choice of color schemes in their clothing. (Danni actually detested the styles they wore, but she was determined to find *something* to compliment about their wardrobes.) She began telling them how honored she was to be their mother, how glad she was when they spent time together, how she prayed for them and thanked God for them every day. The kids actually started sharing with her about their school friends, about their likes and dislikes, about their dreams and fears.

When Danni looked back at what their household had been before she started seriously seeking God, before the family started praying together, she was spiritually aghast. The family had lived most of their lives in what now felt like a barren land. They had wandered around in the same house, attended church, eaten together, and even done "family stuff," but they had not known the supernatural love that God could breathe into their home. Not until they began to pray together as a family. Not until Danni and Brice regularly prayed together as a couple. Not until Danni took the time to truly seek God *with her whole heart.*

What Do You Prefer?

You have a choice: your words will be like either poison ivy or roses. Which one would you rather have fill your home?

Every time you criticize, you plant poison ivy in your home. Every time you praise your family members, you're distributing roses. Each word of encouragement plants beds of fragrant flowers. Your walls will be covered with rose vines, heavy in bloom. Your furniture will be covered with rose petals. Your family will have the blush of roses on their faces, otherwise known as a glow of approval. Your whole life will smell good.

I have seen these "roses" in my own family, but they became more vivid several years ago when I taught junior high school students. I decided that if those teenagers didn't learn anything else from me, they were going to learn the power of praise. Therefore, every day we put the name of one student at the top of the board. Each student in the class would then write something positive or praise-worthy about that student. I then read the compliments out loud. I knew the activity was powerful because of the smile it always put on the face of the one receiving the praise.

But one day the students completely surprised me and put *my* name on the board. A student read the praises out loud. I felt as if that class had woven together a cloak of rose petals and placed it on my shoulders. My spirit "smelled roses" all day long.

The same thing happens when we praise our family. Our words weave together a fragrant cloak that wraps around their souls and gives them a verbal hug from the most influential woman in their lives—their wife or mom. The "roses" I planted in that junior high class eventually produced yards and yards of silky roses for my own shoulders. So the roses we cultivate in our families will result in a spirit of praise that also envelopes the person doing the praising. In other words, if you crave praise, begin praising your family. "In everything, do to others what you would have them do to you, for this sums up the Law and the Prophets" (Matt. 7:12).

Every day I make an effort to tell my children that they're exactly the kind of children I like, and that if they lined up with all the other children in the world, I would choose them. That's why my four-year-old boy now likes to act out this scenario: he grabs his two-year-old sister by the hand and says, "OK, Mom. Here we are. We're in a line. Now you play like you've gotta choose."

So with a big smile on my face, I walk in front of them saying something like "I really need a girl and a boy to take home with me. I'm so lonely and sad without a boy and girl. Now who should I choose?" Then I pretend I've just seen them, and I make a big deal about how cute they are and how they look like just the children for me. The scene always ends with a generous supply of hugs.

I also make a similar effort with my husband, Daniel, by telling him he's just the kind of man I like. Regularly I tell him something like "If you were single and I were single, and you showed up at church for the first time, I'd flirt shamelessly with you until you asked me out on a date." This kind of praise directed to our family reaps praise in return. I hear my praise returned with Brooke's sighing, "Oh," as she hugs me, with Brett's "Mama, you're my best friend," and with Daniel's ready compliments.

Powerful Praise

As destructive as the negative is in our lives, praise, love, and encouragement are more powerful by far. Paul knew this, or otherwise he wouldn't have written, "Whatever is true, whatever is noble, whatever is right, whatever is pure, whatever is lovely, whatever is admirable—if anything is excellent or praiseworthy—think about such things" (Phil. 4:8). Our thoughts affect our actions in some powerful ways. If we're thinking praise, we'll act praise. Remember, this kind of thought life happens only after we allow God to clear our lives of the "dragons." *It's bigger than just being complimentary, because we feel like that's what we're supposed to do.* The most powerful kind of praise flows from the heart and, like Danni, naturally spills from us because we've spent time with the One who's the source for everything positive in the universe.

If we as godly women are going to impact our homes for the Lord, Phil. 4:8 should become our theme for life.

This verse is an excellent one on which to meditate. Our children, whether they're grown or preschoolers, will reflect our attitudes. For instance, when my first child, Brett, was born, I decided I would praise him until I died. By the time he was three it became evident that he was thoroughly in-doctrinated in the art of praise. One day he and I were playing softball in the backyard. He held the bat, and I tossed the ball to him. Repeatedly he missed, but I would say, "That's OK, Brett. Just keep on trying. Keep on trying. You're doing great! Keep trying!"

After about a dozen misses, he looked at me with a positive expression and said, "I'm a good misser!" That kind of attitude will ensure that Brett will believe in himself and his God-given abilities. And praise does make a difference, because now, at the ripe old age of four, Brett has learned to hit the ball across the yard. Now he's a good *hitter!*

Furthermore, if we don't praise our children and give them the respect due all human beings, we can forget their respecting or praising us. According to J. Otis and Gail Led-better in their book *Family Fragrance,* children are due re-spect simply because they are creations of God. This does not mean that we should not discipline them or not expect them to respect us as parents. However, discipline should be carried out in such a way that it preserves the child's dignity and does not degrade.[1] I have found that as long as I praise and encourage my children, they *know* when they have a moment of discipline due them, and they resent the act far less because I have laid a groundwork of the positive.

"Respect is holding other people in honor so they may recognize their own true worth," wrote Noah Webster. Ac-cording to Judy Cornelia Pearson and Paul Edward Nelson in their book *Understanding and Sharing,* self-fulfilling prophecy basically refers to what you tell people, especial-ly children, about themselves is the basis for how they will in fact react. This concept enforces the biblical "power of praise." For instance, if you repeatedly criticize children or complain about them, they will act out more negative behavior, which brings about more criticism or complaining. On the other hand, if a parent praises children and focuses on what's right with them, they'll respond with more positive behavior.[2] In short, praise works. If you want your children to be better behaved, praise them for what good behavior they do display and you'll get even more good behavior from them.

As important as praise is to our children, if we don't respect and praise our husbands in front of the children, whether they are grown or toddlers, we can forget their respecting and praising their father. Our husbands are the God-appointed leaders of our family. They deserve the respect of that position. Likewise, the wife deserves equal respect from her husband because of her God-appointed role as the "atmosphere builder" in the home. When children show disrespect to their father, we wives might say something like "Don't talk about your father that way!" But daily we might talk *to* him as if he doesn't deserve one ounce of praise or respect, or chastise him as if he were one of the children. This will kill a spirit of praise in a home. Just as I modeled praise and respect to my junior high class, these virtues should first be demonstrated between a husband and wife before the children will learn to praise and give respect.

It's very easy to think, "Yeah—but you don't know the beast I'm living with! My husband regularly criticizes me in front of the children. My children are like monsters right now, and I really can't find a thing to praise any of them for." My answer is found in chapter 1. Go back to that chapter and implement each truth from there through chapter 4. Rid your own life of the dragons and seek God seriously on behalf of your family and husband and you'll find that the praise issue is much less of an issue for you. Even if your family is not praising you, *you* praise *them!* "Love your enemies, bless those who curse you, do good to those who hate you, and pray for those who spitefully use you and persecute you," even if those people are in your own family (Matt. 5:44, NKJV).

But be warned! If praise has not been a way of life, when you begin it with your family they most likely will not respond in the way you first expect. If you have habitually criticized and complained and God reverses your attitudes, the first reaction from your husband and children might be suspicion mixed with a statement such as "What's *the matter* with you?" Remember—your home will still be filled with the poison ivy that was "planted" in previous years. Only after you distribute a generous supply of "roses" will your family realize that your new, biblical attitude is not simply a good mood but a new way of life. Pray that God will give you patience with your family, even if they don't immediately recognize the spiritual reformation you're undergoing.

Someone else's shortcomings don't justify our own.

If a family is not praising the wife and mother, if they are bickering, if they are hateful, if they are disrespectful, that does not excuse the wife's lack of praising the family or her active participation in sins of attitude. Sometimes children are merely mirroring the parents' behavior, and the parents can't see it. Therefore, get on your face before God and ask Him to show you something positive about each member of your family that you can praise. Also ask Him to show you if you planted the poison ivy that sprouted in your home and is choking the life out of your family. He *will* show you. Sometimes our family life is in shambles simply because we parents are reaping what we have sown (see Gal. 6:7). If we have sown prayerlessness, we will reap "dragons" and also teach our children how to reap them. When those "dragons" breathe fire at us, we often point fingers at our children when we should be asking God to purify our own lives and create in us a godly example to our families. Not only will God open your eyes to these uncomfortable areas, but He'll also reveal areas in which you can begin praising every family member. The skin tone of your daughter, the hair color of your son, or the smile of your husband—choose to continually compliment, choose to praise!

You are responsible for the atmosphere in your home. You are a representative of the Church to your family. When you start regularly praising them, even if you don't feel like it, you'll see something wonderful and exciting begin to take place. Praise is a principle of God that unleashes His supernatural power into a home.

One of the great heartaches of Christian life is that many families seem to be the best church members and the nicest, most wonderful people outside the home. But after their front door closes, look out! These very same families become nothing short of ferocious beasts, bent on mercilessly devouring one another with sinful words and actions. In other words, their "sin dragons" are at war with each other. It's so easy to fall into this trap because we are familiar with our family and think we can let our guard down with them. If we are where we should be spiritually, the stuff that comes out when we do relax will be holiness, righteousness, and love. Jesus said it with these words:

> No good tree bears bad fruit, nor does a bad tree bear good fruit. Each tree is recognized by its own fruit. People do not pick figs from thornbushes, or grapes from briers. The good man brings good things out of the good stored up in his heart, and the evil man brings evil things out of the evil stored up in his heart. For out of the overflow of his heart his mouth speaks.   —Luke 6:43-45

Sure—there will be some days when you're frustrated and don't feel very holy. That's normal. But our feelings are never an excuse for abandoning biblical principles. This is where God can teach us to exercise self-control and be a praise-giver even when we don't feel like it. When your family life is more like a war zone or the cold war, a wife's choice to praise anyway will often instigate the upward journey toward what is true, noble, right, pure, lovely, admirable, excellent, and praiseworthy (see Phil. 4:8).

None of the previous comments are meant to imply that a wife is in any way responsible for her husband's relationship with God, or vice versa. We are individually responsible before God for our relationship with Jesus Christ. "Work out your own salvation with fear and trembling; for it is God who works in you both to will and to do for His good pleasure" (Phil. 2:12-13, NKJV). Nonetheless, this section is meant to underscore the truth that a mother and wife who *chooses* to set a tone of praise in her home will find that she is creating a spirit of truth that encourages spiritual growth in the whole family.

Furthermore, this is not a lesson in ignoring family problems and pretending they don't exist. That will absolutely never breed a positive spirit of worship in the home. Quite the contrary, brushing problems under the rug, whether in a marriage or in a parent-child relationship, results in frustration, tension, and a strained family. As I've already stated, there's always room for "speaking the truth in love" (Eph. 4:15). But even with a family working through a mound of problems, a spirit of praise will do nothing but good.

Paul sums it up best with "Do not let any unwholesome talk come out of your mouths, but only what is helpful for building others up according to their needs, that it may benefit those who listen" (Eph. 4:29). This means that praise benefits the recipients as well as those who are listening. Therefore, we can *choose* to praise our family both when they're present and when they aren't. For instance, I make it a point regularly, habitually to praise my husband to my children. At the birth of my son and the adoption of my daughter, I pledged that those children would never, *absolutely never,* hear me criticize their father. So whether my husband is present or not, I tell my children things like "You have the best dad in the world. Your daddy is so smart! You're so fortunate to have such a wonderful dad!" Both of them now heartily agree. Praise benefits the listener! This type of praise enables my son and daughter to think, "Yeah—Dad *is* great!" Likewise, I praise my children in front of their father, and to him even when they're not present.

We should not only praise our family but also praise God in front of our family. Say things like "Thank God for the beautiful sunset" or "Praise the Lord for the rain!" or "Look at the stars! Don't they just scream, 'God is awesome!'?" Such conversation continually emphasizes our Lord as the source of all beauty and everything good in us. Indeed, "Every good and perfect gift *is* from above, coming down from the Father of the heavenly lights" (James 1:17, emphasis added). Also, humming prayer choruses or playing worship music weaves a spirit of praise and worship throughout the home that nurtures spiritual growth: our own, our children's, and our husbands'. When we have a daily, radical, soul-searching experience with God almighty, like King David we can have a heart overflowing with praise (see Ps. 63:1-5). In short, a habit of praise won't develop in us unless we're continually seeking God. *The secret to a spirit of praise is coming completely clean with God and allowing Him to give us pure hearts.*

A wife of noble character who can find?
She is worth far more than rubies. . . .
Her children arise and call her blessed;
her husband also, and he praises her:
"Many women do noble things,
but you surpass them all."
Charm is deceptive, and beauty is fleeting;
but a woman who fears the LORD
is to be praised.
—Prov. 31:10, 28-30

Ruby "Am I's"

1. Am I scattering "roses" in my home?
   Evidence that you are: A spirit of praise dominates

your conversations with every member of your family, including your spouse.

2. Am I giving my husband the respect he is due as the head of our household and my spiritual journey mate?

   Evidence that you are: You abstain from criticizing him in front of or to the children, even if they're grown. Any constructive criticism is offered in private with a loving and caring attitude. You regularly praise him in his presence as well as in his absence.

3. Am I doubting the miraculous power of prayer and praise?

   Evidence that you are: While reading this chapter and previous chapters, you have thoughts such as "There's no way this will ever work for my family. We're too far gone!"

4. Am I inhibiting the spirit of praise in my home with negative media input, such as ungodly movies, music, and literature?

   Evidence that you are: You shrink at the idea of a spiritual mentor, such as your pastor, looking through your videotapes, compact discs, and books.

5. Am I focused on what is praiseworthy?

   Evidence that you are: Your first focus is on God. He above all is worthy of praise!

Ruby "Ifs"

1. If you have trouble praising your family:

- Ask God to show you where to start praising.
- Memorize Phil. 4:8, and recite it to yourself every time you start to voice criticism.

2. If you're not negatively influencing your family with ungodly media entertainment, but your husband is:

- Daily intercede for him and pray that God will convict him.
- Look for opportunities for conversations in which you can express your humble, caring, wifely concern.
- Be careful not to nag, but be open to expressing a gentle word in God's timing.

3. If you've been freed of the dragons, and praise is ready on your lips—but you look at your family and see that they are all dragon-infested and negative:

- Intercede for them. I can't say it enough.
- Become a mother who is a prayer warrior and a spiritual powerhouse!
- Remember that God can do anything when we're willing to allow Him to unleash His power in our families and our homes by first allowing Him to unleash His power *in us*.

4. If you have friends who would rather complain and criticize than praise:

- Look for places to steer your conversations toward the positive.
- Pray for them, and ask God to put a network of God-focused friends into your life.
- Unless God shows you otherwise, don't break your friendships with those who are not God-focused, because you'll remove your godly, positive influence from them.
- Watch God perform miracles in their attitudes as they see your righteous example.

> *If we're going to create a godly atmosphere*
> *in our homes, we must be willing to relinquish all*
> *we possess and give it to others should God so ask.*
> *This decidedly frees us from the materialistic*
> *lifestyle and empowers us to revolutionize*
> *our homes and our worlds.*

~6~

Rubies and Poison

▷ Danni's Story

As Danni tapped into the positive power of praise and saw her family blossom in the presence of the Lord, she just knew that she was "there" spiritually. Not that she had "arrived," by any means, but Danni felt God had purged her of so much that there simply couldn't be anything left.

She was wrong. Quietly but forcibly, God began to work on her in another area, a place so culturally ingrained that she never would have seen the flaw without the light of the Holy Spirit on her heart.

In spite of all the biblical admonishments against it, Danni had somehow bought into the cultural concept of materialism. Its subtle vines, so popular in America, had woven right in with the rose vines on her walls. The materialistic mat, as green as fresh dollar bills, presented itself as a beautiful background for the rose blossoms. But the tendrils had the capacity to slowly choke the roses and destroy the godly atmosphere in Danni's home.

The closer Danni got to God, the more He began to lay

His finger on some of her prized possessions and ask her if she would give these away if He were to require it. At first Danni panicked. These tormenting thoughts that she should relinquish everything couldn't be from God! Why would He require that she give away the things in life she loved the most? These possessions were *hers,* not God's, she thought.

Hadn't she been through *enough* with all the spiritual purging God had so far required? Hadn't she been obedient *enough* in changing her focus to God, in her prayer life, in praising her family? But when she got brave enough to pray again, Danni's thoughts again turned to all these things she owned. And she saw in her mind that she held them all in her tight grip, squeezing them for all she was worth. Soon, she realized that she didn't own them—those possessions owned her.

Danni had been so thankful for the roses in her family, those blooms of heady fragrance, which covered her walls and furniture and spread "shine" to her whole household. But God began to show her that mingled with those blooms were other "blooms" that looked beautiful but spewed poison in the Christian soul and tainted the godly atmosphere in a home. The blooms of materialism.

Rappaccini and Materialism

In 1844 Nathaniel Hawthorne wrote a story titled "Rappaccini's Daughter." It details the experience of a young man named Giovanni Guasconti, who lives in Italy. Next door to his new apartment is an exquisite, although unusual, garden that belongs to a scientist named Giacomo Rappaccini. Rappaccini has an incredibly beautiful daughter named Beatrice. The scientist behaves strangely in the garden, afraid to touch any of the plants, and especially "one shrub in particular, set in a marble vase in the midst of the pool, that bore a profusion of purple blossoms, each of which had the luster and richness of a gem." Nonetheless, his daughter Beatrice gladly embraces the gemlike blooms, drinks in their fragrance, and seems immune to the plant's poison, which instantly kills insects and lizards. Enthralled with Beatrice's unmatched beauty, Giovanni visits the garden and begins courting the young woman. Even though the two lovers maintain their distance, Giovanni notices that the unusual odor of Beatrice's breath matches the odor of the poisonous plant's gemlike blossoms. Without realizing it, Giovanni likewise becomes poisonous as well, simply by associating with Beatrice in the garden. And as Beatrice's breath causes flowers to wilt, so Giovanni's breath kills spiders and flies. The story ends on a tragic note, with Beatrice's death and Giovanni's being forced to a life of isolation because he is now poisonous to the real world.[1]

This story illustrates what can happen to Christians who allow the materialistic thought process to poison their souls. Giovanni eventually realizes he is as poisonous as Beatrice and breaks the horrible news to her, then she begins to pray. Upon the heels of her prayer, Giovanni says, "Dost thou pray? . . . Thy very prayers, as they come from thy lips, taint the atmosphere with death."[2] So it is with us! When we're consumed by materialism, our prayers do nothing more than taint the atmosphere of our homes, because they give our children and husbands a warped view of a wife and mother truly committed to the Lord.

Guess what—you cannot serve God and materialism (see Matt. 6:24). The two don't mix. They're like oil and water. For Christian wives and mothers, it's very easy to develop a "churchy" version of the world's view on this. Our culture so indoctrinates us that we often don't even see it. I know. I've been there. Five years ago if you had asked me if I were materialistic, I would have looked you square in the eyes, said a resounding "No!" and sincerely believed I was telling you the truth. After all, because of my financially poor background, I was often generous with those in need, because I have been one in need and understand how it feels.

Generosity and empathy for the poor do not mean a person is not materialistic. Any of us can give to others and tithe on our incomes, then pat ourselves on the backs and think we've done a wonderful job with generosity. *But the bottom line is—how does my view on material possessions contrast with my culture's view?* If there isn't a drastic contrast, then that poisonous purple, "material" flower is present on the walls of the home, mixed right in with the roses. For the Bible makes some radical statements about materialism that are in direct opposition to our culture.

When I got serious with God, He showed me that I was a wife and mother who was allowing materialism to taint the atmosphere of my home.

Material Debra

During the latter half of my childhood, I was poor. My father became the minister of a small church, and the parsonage family didn't have much. But our basic needs were met: food, water, clothing, shelter. Nonetheless, I was surrounded by peers who were lavished with material possessions. This made me determined about one thing: I would be a wealthy adult.

By the time I hit 20, if you gave me three nickels, I could save four. And I began hoarding most of my money. The part I didn't hoard, I spent on "status" items that would bring me recognition among my peers and make me feel that I had worth: nice cars, diamond rings, designer clothing, fancy furniture. My husband and I were at middle income level, but I felt smug in my materialistic accomplishments and "arrived" at church every Sunday ready to impress anyone who noticed my possessions. But despite my smugness, I had a deeper emotion, a voice that demanded more purchases, more money, more luxury to fill an ever-increasing void.

At the same time, I heard a softer voice—one that whispered that there must be more to Christianity. That quiet voice led me on a journey from materialism to faith, which revolutionized my life. It all started when I was 31 and began regularly, seriously seeking God—not just the

obligatory prayer requests that had characterized my former devotion time, but *seeking God.* My "altar" was the side
of my bathtub. That was the only place I could go to escape
my toddler. Leaving my husband in charge, I went into the
bathroom, locked the door, and sat on the side of the tub almost every night. I read scripture and sought God as much
as possible. "Please, God—I want to see You moving in my
life," I prayed one whole autumn. A lot of things began to
happen within me. God led me into confession, repentance,
restitution, and righteousness.

But He also led me down a path I never anticipated. I'll
never forget when He began showing me that path. I was in
a church service and began to feel the overwhelming urgency that I should give to those in need half of what I made
from my writing. I resisted that feeling with a vengeance. After that service, I convinced myself I had been half-crazy to
even have such a thought. Between my husband's job and
my writing career, we were still only middle income, so giving more than my tithe shouldn't have even been an issue. I
scrapped the whole idea.

But it came back every time I was in church. I could
stifle the feeling that I should give sacrificially with the
clamor of daily living, but I couldn't stifle that feeling in
church. To top it all off, one particular Bible verse began to
haunt me: "Sell all that you have and distribute to the poor,
and you will have treasure in heaven; and come, follow
Me" (Luke 18:22, NKJV). If God asked me to give everything I owned to the poor, was I willing to obey? *No!*

Selfishly, I enjoyed my stuff too much to sacrifice it for
anybody. I began to realize, sitting there on the side of my
bathtub, that perhaps I wouldn't see God, really see God,
until I got to the point that He meant more to me than my
material possessions and my money. That persistent tiny
voice that led me to seek God grew into a deafening cho-
rus and confirmed my realization.

I desperately fought the feelings. Oh, how I wrestled
them! If I started giving sacrificially, if I started putting the

needs of the poor as a priority in my heart, I would have to say no to some of my materialistic wants and dreams. I would have to totally change my materialistic thought pattern! I would have to deny that voice within me that said the more I owned the more worthy I would be. No more dreams of a luxury car, no more plans for a fancy home, no more updating perfectly good furniture, no more diamonds, no more buying clothing I didn't really need. The whole notion sent me into a tailspin!

We were planning to adopt internationally. God whispered to me about giving away my adoption fund. Would I be willing to help other couples adopt children and deny my own dreams of adoption? No! I wanted to adopt. Those other orphans couldn't be as important as the child we would adopt. I learned of an orphanage in Russia that was struggling to keep the electricity and phone connected. Would I dare dig into the money I had hoarded for my own adoption and meet the needs of children I would probably never see?

After an intense, internal struggle, I did. And so began my journey from materialistic selfishness to godly selflessness. After several such instances of sacrificial giving, I put up less resistance to that overwhelming, supernatural urgency that I should give until it hurt. By that time, my "bathtub devotion" had moved to the couch and from the couch to on my face before God—if not always literally, always in my heart. In my heart I was on my face before God when I told Him that I would give what He said when He said and to whom He said.

Radical action followed. After yet another vicious, internal struggle, I gave away half of my beloved wardrobe to a friend who had been praying for clothing. These were the status clothes that I had worn to underscore my value in the presence of my peers. I was reminded of Luke 3:11, "He who has two tunics, let him give to him who has none" (NKJV). This is a giving ratio of 50 percent. And I didn't give the half of my wardrobe I disliked—I gave the designer clothing, my absolute favorites, the items I most likely would never be able to replace because of my new standard of giving. I had been so in love with those clothes, so attached to the notion that they increased my worthiness, that the act of giving them was like having my insides ripped out.

But God showed me that when I had given to someone less fortunate the things I didn't want or need, I had not been truly giving. I had been discarding.

Unless I relinquish what I love or need, I have not experienced true giving. According to Mother Teresa, "You must give what will cost you something. This, then, is giving not just what you can live without, but what you can't live without or don't want to live without, something you really like. Then your gift becomes a sacrifice, which will have value before God."[3] After the great wardrobe purge, I was still left with a closet full of clothing. My need for clothing was met. Not my want—my need. And I became content with that.

Very soon I began to be spiritually nauseated by other things in my life. Then I began to see in my heart the human beings in our world who have no food, no clothing, no shelter, no education, no medical care. And I, in my selfish, materialistic thought pattern, had wasted money on things unnecessary and useless. I had been nothing more than a middle-income consumer with the word "Christian" painted across my front door.

What started as my "side of the bathtub" search for God was now a full-blown pilgrimage that opened my eyes to the needs around me. At church. In my neighborhood. In my family. Overseas. I began giving on a level I had never given before, and God began a marvelous deep work in me. I awoke one day to realize that I was content, truly content, with my middle-income home. No more yearning for a larger and better house. I was content, truly content, with my thoroughly used economy car. No more burning desire to buy the best vehicle every two years. And I was excited, truly excited, about the prospect of sacrificially giving to feed the hungry, to educate the poor, to help the blind see. Strangely, I felt more worthy than I had ever felt in my whole life.

Worthy in Christ

I soon realized that the materialistic tendencies within me had very subtle roots. Those tendencies went much deeper than the selfish reverberating of "I want. I want. I want." Materialism is an outward manifestation of a deeper, age-old problem—a problem that transcends the 21st century and manifests itself wherever human beings exist, in any society, at any given time in history—in modern America, in biblical Canaan, in the Greek heyday. For instance, a missionary to Africa was asked to relate the biggest problem he saw among the tribes to which he ministered. His reply was "Materialism. If one villager gets a new roof on his hut, then his neighbors writhe with envy until they, too, can acquire a new roof."

To think I made that same mistake my early adulthood—basing my self-worth on material possessions. It's the same everywhere:

- If I drive this particular car, carriage, or ship, then I will be of worth.
- If I dress in these specific jeans, this gown, or that headdress, then I will be of worth.
- If I own this type of brick home or antebellum mansion or the best-thatched hut, then I will be of worth.

There is sad, sad irony in a woman caught in the materialistic thought process: her every acquaintance suffers. For the materialistic woman not only bases her own self-worth on material possessions but also bases the worth of others on material possessions, including the worth of her own husband, children, and extended relatives. This results in the wealthy receiving more honor, recognition, and prestige than the poor. *However, we should base the worth of our families and ourselves solely on being creations of God.*

Furthermore, this never-ending cycle of "I want . . . I want . . . I want . . ." does nothing to end the ache within, that need to be of worth. The cycle only feeds itself, and with each thing acquired it increases the inward chasm that continually demands more possessions. Only when I started focusing on *Christ* with every ounce of my being did that chasm within me become full, filled with God's Spirit. And the endless, gnawing cycle of needing to buy the newest "everything" ceased.

With the end of that gnawing came the beginning of freedom. When I initiated the internal relinquishment of everything I owned for the cause of Christ, I began to experience a freedom I had never known. Until I was freed of the bondage of materialism, I didn't realize that it was indeed prison—a jail cell, with my possessions as warden. For anything, no matter how small, that we aren't willing to give up is our controller, our taskmaster, our warden. In the 12th century, Bernard of Clairvaux wrote, "Money [and possessions] no more satisfy the hunger of the mind than air supplies the body's need for bread."[4] Free of materialism, I realized that only a releasing of the whole self, of all one owns, only a *pure* relationship with Jesus Christ satisfies the hunger of the mind.

Materialism vs. Faith

After the hunger in my mind was truly filled, I was horrified that I had allowed our materialistic culture to affect me and the atmosphere of my home more than I had allowed the Word of God to render its effect. Daily we see advertisements on billboards, radio, and television that appeal to our need to be of worth, the need that shouts in essence, "More! More! More! The more you own, the more worthy you are!" As a result, many Christians have convinced themselves that Christianity is a "me" religion, an excuse to try to fill that never-ending chasm within the human soul with material possessions. We'll experience neither abundant life (see John 10:10) nor a godly atmosphere in our homes until we're willing to release *everything* we own for the cause of Christ.

In one of Christ's frequently quoted statements, He says, "No one can serve two masters; for either he will hate the one and love the other, or else he will be loyal to one and despise the other. You cannot serve God and mammon" (Matt. 6:24, NKJV). According to John Wesley Wright, recent research suggests the word *mammon* has a Canaanite, rather than Hebrew, root and means "stored goods" or "provisions."[5]

Like modern Americans, biblical Canaanites were city people who depended largely on commerce and trade. John Wesley Wright further states, "It seems clear according to Canaanite beliefs that mammon was a word that represented a whole way of life. It described a whole system built upon the value of possessions and stored goods."[6] Therefore, Jesus' warning about not serving mammon is a warning against a whole thought process of misplaced value that can consume a person and wrench the very life out of her spiritually.

A few verses after Jesus mentions mammon, He further says, "But seek first the kingdom of God and His righteousness, and all these things shall be added to you" (Matt. 6:33, NKJV). Taken out of context, this can mean that if we seek God, He will reward us with all the material things we want. Taken properly in context, however, it means that if we seek God, He will supply our needs, specifically food, water, and clothing (see Matt. 6:31, NKJV). Until we as wives and mothers get to the place we're content with only our most basic needs being met, we won't see the heart of God.

I think that's what Christ meant when He said, "Whoever does not receive the kingdom of God as a little child will by no means enter it" (Mark 10:15, NKJV). Children are born naked, with no possessions. Only when we become totally possessionless before God will we truly see Him. And until we do, we'll never find an end to trying to hush that inward torment that insists we must prove our value with material possessions.

A colleague of the late Mother Teresa, Bert White, states, "I think when you focus on money and property ownership, you go the way of the material world, of the Big, of Up and more. It becomes your agenda and then faith can fly out of the window."[7] In other words, faith and materialism cannot coexist, "for either you will hate the one and love the other, or else you will be loyal to one and despise the other. You cannot serve God and mammon" (Matt. 6:24, NKJV).

No to Materialism, Yes to Faith

Sister Kateri, another who served with Mother Teresa, states, "We let [Jesus] take what He wants from us. . . . If He has given you great wealth, make use of it, try to share it with others, with those who don't have anything. . . . And don't take more than you need."[8] But because of our nagging need to be of worldly worth, this philosophy gets reversed in the minds of materialistic Christians. We say, "With this abundance that God has given me, I'll buy everything I can afford. If there's anything left, I'll give to the needy." The result of this thought pattern? There will be precious little, if anything, left for the needy. In contrast to the world, Christ has called us to accumulate nothing for ourselves. He has called us to sacrifice our wants for the needs of others.

While Christians continue in the materialistic thought process, thousands around the world suffer from malnutrition, blindness, disease, and untimely death. According to Alan Harkey, president of Christian Blind Mission International, "Each year an estimated 500,000 children go blind, primarily due to malnutrition. Such children are often viewed as having no value, as being drains on the already precarious finances of many poor families in developing countries. Therefore, more than half of these children die within two years of losing their sight."[9] For the cost of a special treatment of three vitamin A tablets—75 cents—the progression of a child's blindness can often be reversed. Even so, 500,000 children go blind every year.[10]

An experienced missionary informed me that 53 percent of South Africans live below the $60 a month poverty line, and the South African cost of living is higher than that of the United States. One million South Africans have no access to drinkable water. More than 9 million people in the country live in wretched shacks. Eighty-seven percent of all children in South Africa under the age 12 are nutritionally compromised, and 23 percent suffer from chronic malnutrition. This missionary said she believes what the white, middle-class American doesn't realize is that impoverished people from other cultural backgrounds, like the South African Xhosas, want the same things we want—a safe home, good schools, a yard for their children to play in safely, a rewarding career.

Sometimes we assume that the only things that persons in impoverished cultures should really want (or expect) is a bag of rice and some porridge in a bowl. We're happy to give them that, and it makes us feel that we've done our part. But we forget that we're not satisfied with so little—so why should we expect them to be? They want to have the same things we have—their small piece of the pie. In order to give them that, we have to share our piece—but all we want to give away are the crumbs.

Alan Harkey further states, "When I think about what's not being done for so many of the poor, the words of Jesus cry out in my mind, 'Assuredly, I say to you, inasmuch as you did not do it to one of the least of these, you did not do it to me'" (Matt. 5:45, NKJV).[11] It's not enough that Christian women belong to churches that have programs to feed, clothe, and give to the needy. It's not enough that we dutifully place into the offering plate money we'll never miss. We are called to deny our wants in order to meet the needs of others, to say no to materialism and yes to the faith we need to give sacrificially. This radically shifts the atmosphere of a home and the focus of the family from the "I want" mentality to the heart of Christ.

You might say, "But we're just barely making ends meet. We have no room to give." Materialism is really more about your focus than the *amount* you give. Almost everyone, even the most financially stretched among us, can give. My friend Kim has a one-income household, and she often bakes bread for others. Also recall the widow in Mark 12:41-44, who gave all she had.

We've already seen that materialism is not limited to specific income levels. A person can live below the poverty line and *still be materialistic*. You can be a billionaire who gives away a million dollars a year and *still be materialistic*. You can give double tithe from the minute you are born and *still be materialistic*. Jesus himself said, "Woe to you Pharisees, because you give God a tenth of your mint, rue and all other kinds of garden herbs, but you neglect justice and the *love of God*. You should have practiced the latter without leaving the former undone" (Luke 11:42, emphasis added).

Good deeds, generosity, or a partial obedience to God's Word do not justify an un-Christlike thought process. The questions that determine whether or not I'm materialistic are (1) If Christ literally asked me to sell everything I had for Him, would I be *willing* to do it? and (2) Am I basing my self-worth and the worth of others on the issue of the ownership of wealth?

Christ did not come so Christians could live in luxury. He came first to forgive our sins through His death on the Cross and second to teach us how to pour ourselves out for others. There's a vast difference in having a Christian belief system and literally living Christ (see Luke 6:46-49). Christ himself said, "If anyone desires to come after Me, let him deny himself, and take up his cross, and follow Me" (Matt. 16:24, NKJV). This is a radical reversal of the focus on "me." This type of experience revolutionizes every thought a person has and replaces the materialistic atmosphere of the home with a melody of holiness: Self-sacrifice. I give. I'm content with this. I'm content with that. I'm content with all. Rededicated. Redeemed. Renewed. Happy with only my basic needs met. Christlike.

No Parlor Religion

The point isn't that Christian women should never go shopping, purchase things, or save money. The point is that if we're going to be a powerhouse for Christ in our homes, then we must be *willing* to relinquish all we possess and give it to others should God so ask. This decidedly frees us from the materialistic lifestyle and empowers us to revolutionize our homes.

Christianity is not and can never be a convenient "parlor" religion that we couch in terms of society's materialistic norms. Anything less than a radical purging of every human tendency, of every human value system, falls short of what Christ himself taught. And the only avenue to purging every human tendency and every human value system is daily getting on our face before God, seeking His holiness, His righteousness, His love. Only then can He begin the purging within us, wrap His arms around us, and teach us to see ourselves as valuable because of His love.

> **The irony of the materialistic mind-set: as long as we're chasing rubies and other "status items," we'll not be worth more than rubies to our families.**

God did not create the home and marriage and motherhood so I could sit in the parlor and seek "my" dreams for the future, "my" dreams of a career, or "my" dreams of material possessions. God did not create us to buy everything we could afford. God created us to have the faith to seek *Him* and be satisfied with *Him*. Only when we seek Him with our whole heart can He then thoroughly implant himself within us and show us dreams that will fit us better than any we could ever imagine. Only after we lose ourselves and our possessions completely to Him will we truly find ourselves (see Matt. 10:39) and end that gnawing human dilemma of basing our worth on what we own. We will find our worth in Him. The Christian woman who is willing to abandon herself to Christ to this level should not be the exception. That woman should be the norm.

The Balance

Realize that there's a balance when being content with only what we need. For instance, one of the things that turns a house into a home is a mother's desire to make it attractive for her family and guests. My family and I could live without the decorations in our home, as could you and your family. But those decorations, along with the burning candles and rugs on the floor and other things, create an atmosphere of beauty and serenity to make our home inviting (see J. Otis and Gail Ledbetter, *Family Fragrance*).

The same balance must be achieved in the physical appearance of wives and mothers. While we all can *live* without makeup or an up-to-date haircut, we owe it to our family to spend a few dollars on making ourselves attractive and, as Patsy Clairmont says, "lookin' good," when at all possible.[12] According to Willard F. Harley, one of a husband's top five needs is for an attractive wife.[13] In other words, a man needs a wife who has taken proper time for grooming and self-care. I confirmed this recently when I told my husband that I thought I might just go to church without makeup. And my low-key, unassuming "hunk" husband informed me that if I went to church without wearing makeup, he would hyperventilate. Enough said!

▷ **Danni's Story**

At long last, Danni mustered up the nerve to tell the Lord that she would give away *everything* for Him should He ask. *Everything*. Right down to her engagement ring and her designer socks. That's when God released her, and like Abraham when he was planning to sacrifice Isaac (see Gen. 22:1-19), Danni knew that God wasn't asking her to literally give everything away. He was asking her to value Him more than her possessions, so much more that her

possessions paled to nothingness next to her love for the
Lord. She realized that God really *did* want to blow her
socks off with His power, but she had been too busy hanging onto those socks because they were, after all, *designer*
socks and cost *money!*

At long last she began to see the world, *really* see the
world, through the eyes of her Lord, not through the materialistic "binoculars" of her culture. She soon found that
she valued people equally—the street person, the prosti-
tute, and the millionaire—because they were creations of
God. That meant she also valued her family on a new level, with true unconditional love.

> **A wife of noble character who can find?**
> **She is worth far more than rubies. . . .**
> **She opens her arms to the poor and**
> **extends her hands to the needy.**

                      —Prov. 31:10, 20

Ruby "Am I's"

1. Am I materialistic?
   Evidence that you are: You're not willing to sell all you
   have and give to the poor, should God so ask. You base
   your self-worth and the worth of others on the issue of
   the ownership of wealth and/or social status.

2. Am I teaching my children to be materialistic?
   Evidence that you are: You are materialistic; they learn
   by watching you. Or, if you aren't materialistic, they
   could be learning simply from the American culture. If
   you're not teaching them *not* to be materialistic, they
   most likely will be, simply from association.

3. Am I creating a materialistic atmosphere in my home?
   Evidence that you are: If something of value accidentally gets broken, you're more concerned with the broken possession than with the feelings of the child or

person who accidentally broke it. You lambaste the offender at the expense of wounding his or her spirit. You often buy items you don't need simply to get a materialistic "thrill" from the new possession. During holidays, you encourage your husband to overspend for your wants and never consider the millions of wives and mothers in the world with no food, clothing, or shelter for themselves or their children. You often go into debt for items you don't need simply to keep up with the trends.

4. Am I radically, totally committed to God?

Evidence that you are: There's nothing, no person, or possession or dream you hold more dear than Him. You feel a freeing release from your possessions and are also more free in your relationships than you have ever been because you're not trying to hold onto or control people or possessions.

Ruby "Ifs"

1. If you're materialistic:

- Ask God to purge you. This is going to hurt! God will most likely require that you begin a cycle of giving, as He did me. You will know God's voice by the biblical thoughts that enter your mind, especially when you're trying to pray.

2. If you aren't materialistic, but your husband is:

- Pray for him.
- Model, but don't preach, a giving attitude to him. For instance, at Christmas, request that he give most of the money he would spend on you to a reputable organization that cares for the needy. Then ask for a Christmas present that reflects a need in your life, rather than a want. Also realize that there must be a balance. If I become totally focused on not having material possessions, that, too, can be a manifestation of materialism, because my attention is still on the material. It all boils down to what I'm pursuing in life. Am I pursuing God, or am I pursuing material possessions? Or (read this slowly) am I just trying to create the image of pursuing God by reducing my material possessions so I look good to those around me? God wants us to be free of the restraints of the world and dependent on Him, at which we're willing to sell every possession if He should ask. This type of devotion to our Creator will revolutionize the atmosphere in our homes.

> *Trying to create a godly atmosphere in the home*
> *while doing the work of three women is like trying*
> *to steer a small boat that has a two-ton anchor*
> *attached to it: it's an impossible task.*

~7~

Rubies and Boats

▷ Danni's Story

Danni had a problem—a real problem. She was over-committed. She spent her days running around trying to fulfill a list of extra duties to which she had obligated herself at church, at her part-time job, at her son and daughter's high school. In short, she had tried to be "Supermom" for many years. If there was a job to be done, everybody knew they could count on sweet, self-sacrificing Danni.

One morning she got up, looked in the mirror, and saw herself in a new way. In reality, she wasn't even sure she knew the person in the reflection. Danni had been so busy being busy for such a long time that she suddenly felt as if she had been running from something deep within. She wasn't sure what that something could be, but it certainly hurt. Just thinking of the whole thing sent a hot tear streaming down her cheek. Trembling, Danni collapsed onto her bed, suddenly weary with the thought that she was facing yet another busy day. Was she living life, or was life living her? How long had it been since she felt truly in control of her life?

One thing was certain: Danni needed a break. But today was supposed to be one of the busiest days in weeks! The church committee, the hours at work, the planning of the junior-senior banquet at school. All at once she felt exhausted, and the day hadn't even started.

How was she supposed to be an instrument through which the Lord could create a godly atmosphere in her home? She always felt as if she were running off in all directions. True—her prayer life had become nothing short of miraculous. With God's help, she had expelled the dragons from her life. The family was closer to one another than they had ever been, more like a team and less like a group of individuals living under the same roof. Her marriage had drastically improved, just from those regular hours she and Brice spent together with God.

God was definitely first with Danni. But this morning some inner voice showed Danni that it could all be much, much better if she would simply put her family as a firm second in her life and quit trying to prove herself through a host of high-profile activities.

Even though her day was horribly busy, Danni wasn't able to drown the new awareness of pain from her thoughts. All day, she felt a new ache she had never experienced before, as if God had brushed aside a pile of dried leaves within her to reveal a gaping hole in the bottom of her soul. And He began to show her that all her busyness was nothing more than an attempt to hide a nagging feeling that she was not of worth, that her position as mother and wife was somehow less than important.

In her mind Danni repeatedly saw herself as the "star" this, the head of that, the one with it all together. Yet in her mind a childlike, doubtful voice kept saying, "See me! I'm of worth! I *do* matter in the world. I really *do* . . . I *do* . . . Don't I?" And Danni began thinking back to her childhood to see some wounds—some very deep wounds—that she had pretended didn't exist. At the end of that day she collapsed in the corner of her bathroom. Brice found her silently sobbing into a towel.

Row, Row, Row Your Boat

Like Danni, many women fall into the workaholic trap because of feelings of inferiority. In *What Wives Wish Their Husbands Knew About Women,* James Dobson says feelings of inferiority plague most women and are the leading cause of depression. So in order to feel of worth, wives and mothers often take on the jobs of three women, as if by receiving the applause of peers we can make those nagging feelings of inferiority disappear.[1]

Trying to create a godly atmosphere in the home while doing the work of three women is like trying to steer a small boat that has a two-ton anchor attached to it: it's an impossible task. Imagine you and your whole family sitting in a boat. You're afloat near the muddy banks. Your husband is at the boat's bow, binoculars to his eyes, scouting out the lake, trying to decide the best possible spot for your family's outing. At long last he says, "There's where I want to go" and points toward a lovely, shimmering, peaceful haven. You're sitting in the back of the boat, the steering wheel in front of you, and you heartily agree that you want to be smack in the middle of that beautiful spot. Your children, sitting between you and your husband, eagerly cheer your decision. Your job is to steer the boat toward your destination.

But guess what? The end of your boat is stuck in the mud because of the two-ton anchor holding it down. You created the anchor out of busyness, and it is attached to the boat with chains—iron links of inferiority. Those chains drape across the gunwales, wrapping around your legs, your waist, your arms, restricting your every movement. You can't even see the piece of iron that holds you fast, but it's your master. So instead of enjoying the peaceful haven, your family sits in the muddy waters near the bank while God really has something wonderful prepared for you in the haven across the lake.

Your husband keeps starting the boat motor and giving it gas, but he gets nowhere. At long last, out of frustration, he stops and becomes resentful and frustrated. You're frustrated as well and start resenting him. The children pick up on your vibes and start resenting both their mother and their father as well as each other. Eventually a dense fog of resentment settles around your boat, and you can't even see the haven God prepared for you. Furthermore, you're so aggravated and grouchy from being stressed out by doing too much that you daily spread "slime bubbles" all over everyone in your household. At last you forget the haven even exists and decide this is just the best a family gets. What a tragic, horrid, sad situation! But any home with a wife who has taken on too many responsibilities is in such a boat, stuck in the mud.

Please don't feel that I'm saying all problems in a family stem from the wife's lack of fulfilling her biblical role. Quite the contrary! Suppose you have no anchor whatsoever and are willing to steer the family toward the haven, but your husband refuses to crank the engine. Now that's an equally tragic problem. If the family is to maintain any spirituality at all, the wife will be forced to man the engine *and* steer, which can result in the family drifting off course or going around in circles miles away from the destination you so desperately desire to reach.

Rethinking the Roles

One person in a household is not more important than another. It's very easy for both women and men to start thinking that because the man is the leader (the "engine man") he is the most important. That simply isn't true. We fall into this trap because when we sit in this "boat" called the family, we all face forward and look toward the leader, the husband, the "engine man." Since we're all facing the front, we tend to forget the vitally important work the wife is doing in the back of the boat. Furthermore, our society often brainwashes us into believing that a woman's roles are not as significant as a man's. Dobson states, "The traditional roles of women have become matters of disrespect and ridicule. Raising children and maintaining a home hold very little social status in most areas of the country, and women who are cast into that role often look at themselves with unconcealed disenchantment."[2] As a result, women can easily fall into the "overworking to feel important" trap.

On the other hand, I've found that in an attempt to thwart modern society's concept for the roles of women, some churches make women feel that they are of lesser importance than their husbands. This comes from a twisting of scripture such as the verses found in Eph. 5. Note that verse 21 commands *everyone* to "submit to one another out of reverence for Christ," that means wives and husbands. Then verse 22 tells wives to submit to their husbands, and verse 25 tells "husbands, love your wives, just as Christ loved the church." This requires equal submission between husbands and wives. There's no room for a man or a church group to demean a wife or use her as a doormat. Furthermore, as stated in chapter 2, there's no room for a wife to demean her husband or use *him* as a doormat either. On the contrary, if a man is truly loving his wife as Christ loved the Church, he will sacrificially put her best interest above his own, which is exactly the kind of submissive love that Christ poured out on the Cross.

I'm not saying that men are not the head of the household. What I *am* saying is that men should be a *biblical, Christlike* head of the household. This type of head has no need to *tell* his wife to follow him or submit to him, because she'll be so inspired and awed by his walk with the Lord and his spiritual depth that she'll automatically want to steer that family boat wherever he leads. True leadership occurs only when people are *inspired* to follow, not when they're *forced* to follow or are told they *have* to. (See Bryan Chapell, *Each for the Other*. Also see Mark R. Littleton, *Submission Is for Husbands Too,* and Gary Smalley, *Love Is a Decision.*)

But biblically based husband-wife submission is not the case in many households or churches. I've been in discussions about the roles of men and women that left me deflated. The undercurrent was that no way could I as a woman ever "achieve" the spirituality of a man or know God on the level a man knows Him—and that the Lord deliberately honors men more than women. This sometimes comes forth in blatant statements, and it sometimes comes forth in not giving equal time to addressing the issue of a woman's spiritual roles in the home. I think it's partly because many churches and speakers are afraid they'll sound as if they're supporting society's feminist views. How sad that because of this, Christian women can become spiritually anemic. No one has ever told them just how worthy they are as women and how powerful they can be in their God-ordained roles.

Therefore, the belief that women are to be "lessers" spiritually or otherwise is just as unbiblical and untrue as society's view that women are "lessers" if they choose to be homemakers. According to James Dobson, the Russian government abandoned its child-care network because they concluded that feminine responsibilities are so vital to the next generation, the future of their nation actually depends on how they see their women.[3] "The hand that rocks the cradle rules the world"—but only if those hands *take the time* to rock the cradle.

In truth, a wife and mother is the *most* important when she strives to fulfill her own God-created, spiritual role. And the No. 1 requirement for that role is that a woman of God does everything in her power to live intimately with Him and allow Him to transform her into a spiritual powerhouse. "Being the Church" to a family will take every ounce of spiritual force that God imparts to a woman. Likewise, a man is the *most* important when he strives to fulfill his own God-created, spiritual role, not when he's out conquering corporate America or even ignoring the family to "serve God." And he can truly fulfill this role only when he allows God to turn him into a spiritual powerhouse. Together these divergent but equally important roles deliver a dynamic and

influential punch to our society, our homes, and future ~~gen~~
erations.

In other words, regardless of how many books I have
in print or how many people I speak to, I'm at the height of
importance and influence when I'm with my two small children, sitting in the backyard under a tent made from sheets
and sticks, pretending to eat pinecones and hot sauce;
when I'm snuggled in bed with my children to read Bible
stories to them; when I open our day with prayer; when my
husband and I share an early-morning hug and, while still
in each other's arms, we pray together. These are the real
treasures in life. Not money. Not prestige. Not recognition.
All other achievements pale compared to the time I spend
on my knees and the time I spend with my family. And I
must make certain my schedule allows me the freedom to
do what God created me for in the first place.

Rethinking the List

Whether we realize it or not, each of us has a priority
list in our minds. That list can either be biblically based or
based on other influences in our lives—for instance, society or our own inferiority. The biblically based priority list
looks like this: God, family, service to God, career.

1. **God.** "Love the Lord your God with all your heart
and with all your soul and with all your mind" (Matt.
22:37). The Lord must be tops—period. If this isn't the
case, everything else in life will be out of balance, and we'll
be carrying around a collection of "dragon" sins with us
everywhere we go.

2. **Family.** One of the first things God created was the
family. Therefore, the needs of our family come immediately after our relationship with God. This includes our relationship with our spouses. Within this context, the first
family need that should be addressed is the spiritual. The
second is the physical. So if I have only 10 minutes with
my children before we leave for some destination and must
choose whether I pray with them or scrub the bathtub, I
choose prayer.

118 MORE THAN RUBIES

My husband has taken a strong lead in our home on
this issue. I have watched him repeatedly turn down op-
tional overtime at work or excellent job opportunities because it will take away from his fellowship with our family.
This inspires me to do the same with my writing and
speaking. Together, my husband and I have decided that
before we will sacrifice time with our family, we will sell all
we have, rent a shack, and eat beans. There's no negotia-
tion on this issue. We have made the choice not to sacrifice
our family. Indeed—it is a *choice*. Often both men and
women will say, "But I have to work these long hours at my
job to provide for my family." First, make sure the sacrifice
is made to provide for the family and not to be able to buy
a new car every two years or stay in a specific home or
neighborhood, and/or to be inundated with life's "extras."
*Children can physically, emotionally, and spiritually sur-
vive without material extras. Children cannot emotionally
and spiritually survive without their parents' taking time to
continually nurture them.* Furthermore, make sure you
have seriously prayed about God's choices for you and
your family. Our physical standard of living is not nearly as
important as our spiritual and familial standard of living.

I understand there are certain jobs such as firemen or
doctors or evangelists that require time away from the
family. I'm deeply thankful for the people who fill these
roles. However, make certain that time away from the family is not both excessive and continual. A workaholic saying, "I have to work these long hours," is like an alcoholic
saying, "I have to drink to stay alive."

3. Service to God. Service to God includes church attendance and church-related activities, such as teaching
Sunday School, singing in the choir, or witnessing to non-
Christians. Sometimes we think that service to God equals
knowing God. It's often much easier for us to chase
around performing a hundred church-related activities than
it is for us to take time to sit at the feet of our Lord. God
wants us to sit first. At that point He will instruct us as to
what He expects us to *do*.

Recall the story of Martha and Mary in Luke 10:7 Through the years I've heard all sorts of analyses, some of them humorous, of how this story reflects the differing personalities of these women. I'm not going to argue against the different personality types of Mary and Martha. But I will point out several important truths that can apply to our own priorities. First, regardless of personality type, sitting at the feet of Jesus—not giving service to Jesus—should be top priority. Jesus himself referred to this when he said to Martha, "Only one thing is needed" (v. 42). Second, sitting at Jesus' feet is the result of a choice, not a personality type. Jesus said, "Mary has *chosen* what is better, and it will not be taken away from her" (v. 42, emphasis mine). This statement further underscores that sitting at Jesus' feet is more important than serving Him. Furthermore, Jesus' statement stresses that Mary, regardless of her personality type, made a *choice,* a decision of *the will.* After she made that choice, the experience could not be taken from her. She learned something from sitting with and being with Jesus that she never would have learned by being overcommitted.

It's easy to defend Martha here and say, "Yes, but if she hadn't prepared the food, no one would have eaten." That isn't even the point of this story. The point is an issue of *priority.* Sure, I have to cook for my family, do the laundry, scrub the toilets—all that stuff. Sure, I have to study the Sunday School lesson I teach. But none of those things should come before sitting at Jesus' feet—absolutely none of them!

As humble as Jesus was and as many miracles as He performed, I would guess that if Martha had *chosen* to sit at Jesus' feet and, as a result, gotten behind in her chores, Jesus would have either helped her or turned one loaf of bread into enough to feed all the guests. *So many times we get so busy serving the Lord that we don't realize we're actually serving ourselves, trying to achieve importance or make ourselves feel less inferior.* But if we'll simply seek

Jesus Christ first, He'll help us serve Him. And not only will He help us, but He will show us the specific areas in which He wants us to serve. This stops us from attempting to do it all. Furthermore, sitting at Jesus' feet makes us feel more worthy than we could ever feel while trying to do it all. I'm convinced that Martha would have experienced all of these life-changing principles if she had simply possessed Mary's *priorities*.

4. Career. For the most part, the outcome of our careers is to provide for our families. However, whether male or female, we should never, absolutely never, sacrifice our family for our career. Likewise, we should put spiritually related issues such as serving God as a priority over the physical issues in our lives. This results in finding more value serving the Lord than in a career.

Furthermore, remember that our primary service to God occurs when we fulfill His divine calling to our own families. Note that the virtuous woman's lack of idleness is directly related to "watch[ing] over the affairs of her household" (Prov. 31:27), not chasing around after a bazillion jobs outside the household. Her attention to her household, the first of which much be spiritual issues, results in "her children arise and call her blessed; her husband also, and he praises her" (v. 28). This does not mean that she doesn't perform other tasks. She does have her own at-home career. However, it does mean that she has put her family at the top of her priority list, second only to God, and is not sacrificing them for any other interests.

What this biblically based priority list means for me is that my first goal in life is to *seek God,* to know His heart, to sit at His feet as did Mary. My second goal in life is twofold: to nurture my relationship with my husband and to make sure my family sees the Lord in me through all I do. My third goal is to serve the Lord through my writing and speaking career.

When we truly seek God, He will bring order to our lives and direct us in the paths He wants us to go. If you're chasing around doing a million things, I urge you to seek God about *His* plans for your time.

▷ Danni's Story

After Brice found Danni sitting in the bathroom sobbing, he gently lifted her to her feet and held her. In a torrent of words and tears, Danni began to pour out her feelings of inferiority and how she had been doing too much to seek the approval and recognition she craved. After Brice completely understood Danni's problem, he supported her in her decision to cut back most of the activities that had been hindering her from ministering to her own family. Likewise, he saw that he needed to refocus in this area and agreed to reduce some of his own busyness. Together, they shared with their teenagers their desire to put their family first. They even planned a weekly family night in which they began praying and playing together.

Danni felt more peaceful than she had ever felt in her life. However, she realized that before she could fully comprehend how to steer their family's "boat" in the direction God wanted, she must allow God to begin healing some wounds deep within, inflicted long ago.

A wife of noble character who can find?
She is worth far more than rubies . . .
She watches over the affairs of her household
and [because of this] does not eat
the bread of idleness.
Her children arise and call her blessed;
her husband also, and he praises her:
"Many women do noble things,
but you [who have put God as an
absolute first] surpass them all."

 —Prov. 31:10, 27-29

Ruby "Am I's"

1. Am I overworking in order to cover feelings of inferiority?

    Evidence that you are: Deep within, you have a nagging feeling that you're not of worth and that the more you do the more worthy you will be. Therefore, your outside commitments keep you so busy you barely have time to maintain a relationship with your family or create a godly atmosphere in the home.

2. Am I allowing society's view of me to determine how I feel about myself?

    Evidence that you are: You're more interested in what the rest of the world is doing and keeping up with them than you are in aligning your life to biblical standards.

3. Am I allowing a twisted interpretation of the scripture to make me feel that it is acceptable for me to be spiritually weak?

    Evidence that you are: You cling to the idea that because you are female it is less important for you to be spiritually strong.

4. Am I hindering my husband in his leadership role of our home?

    Evidence that you are: You're allowing chains of inferiority to anchor your family's "boat" with your excessive activities. So no matter how much your husband presses the boat's accelerator pedal, the atmosphere in your home remains "blah."

5. Am I "sliming" my family with my grouchiness because I'm exhausted from overworking?

    Evidence that you are: All you want to do when you get home is be by yourself so you can get some rest. The thought of trying to be sweet to your family makes you want to groan, because you are so tired you don't have the energy to move, let alone interact with the family.

6. Am I living the priorities God wants me to live?

    Evidence that you are: You put God first, family second, service to God third, and career fourth. You make no excuses about sitting at Jesus' feet. Likewise, you make no excuses about spending time with your family. You most likely have drastically reduced your outside commitments to a few manageable, *God-appointed* duties.

Ruby "Ifs"

1. **If you're overworking in order to compensate for feelings of inferiority:**
   - Begin to seek God about the issue. Ask God to show you why you feel inferior. Then ask Him to begin healing that wound.
   - When attacks of inferiority come upon you, envision yourself kneeling before God, hands lifted to His loving, adoring face, with a shaft of light encompassing you. Think of that light as His unconditional approval and love.
   - Realize that no amount of human recognition you receive will abate your feelings of inferiority. Only by allowing God to heal the wounds that have caused your inferior feelings can you experience freedom from the endless need to stay busy.

2. **If your husband expects you to overwork:**
   - Ask him to read *What Wives Wish Their Husbands Knew About Women* by James Dobson (Tyndale House, 1975). While he's reading the book, pray like crazy that God will soften his heart and speak to his mind. If he refuses to read it, continue to pray for him and gently explain that if you slow your pace, you can be a better wife and mother. If that doesn't work, ask your physician or pastor to talk with your husband.

3. **If your husband is a workaholic:**
   - Begin praying that he will see his problem. Also pray for an opportunity to lovingly confront him. I know of one specific incident in which a three-year prayer vigil completely reversed the situation. Don't give up!

4. **If your husband thinks his spiritual role is more valuable than yours:**
   - Have him read *Each for the Other,* by Bryan Chapell, and *Love Is a Decision,* by Gary Smalley. And—you guessed it—pray!

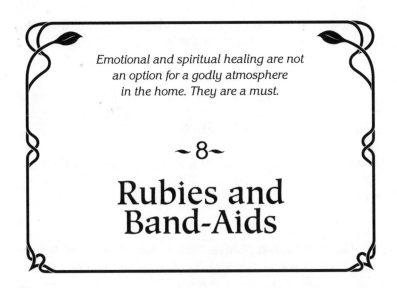

Emotional and spiritual healing are not an option for a godly atmosphere in the home. They are a must.

~8~

Rubies and Band-Aids

▷ Danni's Story

Danni was a woman with a past, and that past had left some very deep wounds within her soul. Without realizing it, Danni had tried to patch some of those serious injuries with nothing more than a "Band-Aid" in order to just get on with life. Now God was removing those "Band-Aids" and offering to heal the wounds.

Some injuries had been inflicted by her parents, some by her peers in childhood and adulthood, some by her relatives, and some even by Brice. She surrendered them one by one, allowing God to gently peel away her attempts to cover them. Danni soon realized that each of her Band-Aids had done nothing but prohibit the wounds from healing. She had covered her pain, and by covering it, she had actually stopped the healing available from God.

Sometimes the healing included gently and lovingly discussing the situation with the person who inflicted the wound and telling that person she forgave him or her. Sometimes it included simply embracing the Lord and allowing Him to impart His supernatural forgiveness through her. Sometimes healing meant asking Brice to change the way he treated her. But it never meant leaving the wound covered.

As Danni allowed her Savior to heal her wounds one at a time, she experienced a new freedom. Actually it was more than freedom—it was deliverance. At long last Danni was truly able to represent the Church to her family, to embrace her life, to value herself for who she was in Christ, not in society, and to spend her life intimately walking with the Savior.

Wounds, Time, and God

The well-known phrase "time heals all wounds" is not totally true. Time never heals spiritual wounds. Only God heals wounds of the mind and soul. If He is left out, time only intensifies the wound, especially when we cover it with unforgiveness.

The "Band-Aid" of unforgiveness works more like a piece of sandpaper than a protector—the longer unforgiveness is harbored, the more it rubs the wound. The wound continues to deepen. The deeper the infection, the broader the wound. Eventually the gaping sore turns into a cancer, rendering a person spiritually void.

The "Band-Aid" of workaholism increases the wound's pain as well. The infection creates a never-ending cycle in a woman's life that says, "I'm not of worth unless I do . . ." The longer this thought process goes on, the more the feelings of inferiority will grow. The more those negative feelings grow, the more deeply a woman is convinced that she really is not of worth. The longer she stays convinced of this falsehood, the more difficult the reversal of the thought process.

The "Band-Aid" of negative behavior only pushes away those we love the most. We might pretend to be tough and independent or have an awful attitude or critical and complaining spirit. As long as we can cover the truth that we're frail human beings who desperately need to depend on God, we perpetuate the lie that says we've got it all together. Other negative behaviors can include food addiction, drug addictions, and raging.

None of these Band-Aids does anything to promote a godly atmosphere in a home. They only hinder spiritual growth and annihilate any chances that God's Spirit will permeate a home through the wife. These Band-Aids also create boundaries between a woman and God, a woman and her husband, and a woman and her children. If a Band-Aid has been placed on your heart, it affects every relationship in which you're involved. No one can "open up and share" with a woman of many Band-Aids, because those Band-Aids are intended to keep everyone, even her own family and God, at arm's length.

Right now I want you to stop and check your pulse. Just put down this book and see if you feel a heartbeat in your wrist.

Did you feel a pulse? If so, that means *you're alive.* Some days, that has been a doubtful question for me! But because you're alive, you most likely have been wounded at some time in your life. You're in good company. Along with me, most every woman reading this book has also been injured somehow. It's part of being human. Somehow, we erroneously think that pain is an isolated incident that "just happened to me." We become very ashamed of our pain and want to cover it with "Band-Aids" because we're certain all the other women we see "have it all together." Guess what? They don't. I don't. You don't. *We're all in the process of allowing God to get it all together for us.*

Realize that the pain in your life will never be healed until you allow God to daily embrace you and begin the healing process. "He heals the brokenhearted and binds up their wounds" (Ps. 147:3). And only by daily spending time in the arms of God can a woman begin to experience emotional and spiritual healing. If a woman is to be an instrument of God in her home, it's imperative that she allow God to begin healing her.

Furthermore, when deep wounds of the spirit occur, issues of low self-esteem always accompany the wounds. Always. The subliminal thought process goes like this, "If I were of worth, that person would have never treated me so despicably. I therefore base my self-worth on past wounds rather than on my eternal worth in Christ." Low self-esteem causes a woman to always focus on herself and prohibits her from focusing on God because of her self-focus. The result is a home not charged with God's power.

> **Emotional and spiritual healing are not an option for a godly atmosphere in the home. They are a must.**

Embracing the Healing

Excellent resources on emotional healing are available in the Christian market. I recommend any of a number of books by David Seamands and Sandra D. Wilson. But I also want to share with you some facts that I've learned about emotional and spiritual healing.

First, you must recognize that you need to be healed. If you've experienced any of the following situations, then you're in need of emotional and/or spiritual healing:

- A divorce (you or your parents)
- Sexual abuse
- Verbal abuse
- Physical abuse
- Rejection by a parent who played favorites
- An emotionally rigid parent
- An absentee parent
- An aloof parent
- The death of a parent during your childhood
- A church or husband that devalues women
- A church that paints a warped image of a God who is more judgment than grace

The telltale sign of any of these situations is usually feelings of inferiority. That within itself is a symptom that some deeper wound exists. *As long as we're in denial, God can't work on us.*

As noted in the list, if you have a concept of God that is erroneous, such as that He's hanging over you, just waiting until you sin so He can gleefully punch you, then you desperately need spiritual healing, and most likely emotional healing. We tend to paint God in the image of our parents. So if your parents were perfectionist and critical with you, then you most likely think that God is the same way and that no matter what you do, it's never good enough. None of this accurately portrays the God of the Bible (read Ps. 103).

If you recognize that you are covered with these kinds of Band-Aids, purchase the books by Seamands and Wilson. Read them. Work through your pain. Allow God to walk you through the issues. My "walking through" took about three or four years. But during all that walking, I kept wondering, "How will I know when God is healing me? What are the characteristics?" Willingness to walk through the pain denotes the beginning of healing. But there are some other signs that God is in the process of healing you. Based on my own experience, here's what I learned:

You know God is healing you when . . .

1. **You have begun the journey of forgiving the person who injured you.** Depending on the depth of the injury, this can take a few days or a few years. Don't think you can ever create a godly atmosphere in your home when you harbor unforgiveness. The woman who harbors unforgiveness creates the atmosphere of bitterness and resentment in her home. Eventually the children will turn that very attitude to her.

I have experienced forgiveness on a very deep level. It's wonderful. It's lasting. It's of God. Don't cheapen God's power in giving you strength to forgive. He's ready and available to give you the courage to relinquish the whole ordeal to Him, which will result in freedom from the past.

2. You can talk about the issues that once gave you great pain. I knew God was intensifying my healing when I had the strength to share the pain of my sexual abuse with a group of women at a shelter for the battered and abused. Two years before that, I never could have spoken the words. But God at last healed me to the point that He could turn my pain into the initiation of healing for others.

3. You feel no need to emotionally isolate yourself from your family and friends. Those who are not embracing God's healing run from emotional intimacy with anyone, including God. You see, the Band-Aids are intact and present a barrier to the world.

4. You have followed Jesus' words to "get up" and "take your mat" with you. In Matt. 9:1-8 Jesus heals a paralyzed man and tells him, "Get up, take your mat and go home" (v. 6). There comes a point in our healing when we must quit wallowing in the past and allowing it to paralyze us spiritually and emotionally. You can spend your whole life reliving the pain if you so choose, and it can eventually become a crutch that stops all emotional and spiritual growth. While it's important to take the time to walk through the pain, which can frequently take several years, we should never stay in the pain our whole lives. This is a deep concern of mine, because we hear so many people exploring their pasts—and then staying there. Regardless of the pain and agony life has dealt us, there comes a time to put the past behind us and allow God to make us a radical influence on the here and now. If we're going to impact our homes for Christ, we must be willing to emulate Paul when he said, "Forgetting what is behind and straining toward what is ahead, I press on toward the goal to win the prize for which God has called me heavenward in Christ Jesus" (Phil. 3:13-14).

Don't think I'm trying to cheapen the pain you've experienced. There have been many times I have felt as if my spiritual and emotional guts had been ripped out. We must never sweep pain under the rug or put Band-Aids over it and deny our wounds. In order to heal, we visit the past. But we also must never stay there. If our homes are to be permeated with God's presence because of our powerful relationship with Him, we cannot afford to allow the past to cripple us. As godly women, we must grit our teeth, pray for God's strength, pick up our mats, and *walk*. Not limp, not hobble, not crawl—but walk, upright, sure-footed, and in love with the One who has delivered and healed us. (See Heb. 12:1-3.)

5. Finally, you know you're embracing healing when you've rewritten your story. In contrast, examine these words by author Wayne Muller:

> After many years, our habitual ways of seeing ourselves become so chronic that we can hardly imagine any others. We are no longer simply a child, a human being; we have become the Unloved, the Vulnerable, the Disappointed One, the Abandoned, the Misunderstood, the Deprived, the Terribly Broken. Waking up in the morning and getting ready for the day, we put on our story like an old bathrobe and a soft pair of slippers. We are so accustomed to introducing ourselves as the victim of our story, we actually feel ambivalent about whether or not we can really change—or even want to. Our very life becomes a familiar, droning habit.[1]

> *It was good for me to be afflicted so that*
> *I might learn your decrees.*
> —Ps. 119:71

For me, rewriting my story meant defining myself by who I am in Christ, not by what has been in the past or what I have accomplished in the present or even by what my future might hold. Only one thing stands firm, and it is this—Jesus Christ died for me. God the Father loves me *so much* that He stepped from eternity and broke into our world to express His love in the form of His Son, sacrificially given for my sins. God did not extend himself in sacrifice so that I can hobble along in spiritual defeat, defining myself by what others say or by my past. Given that truth, I will *not* live in spiritual defeat. I will *not* allow Satan a foothold in my life. I will *not* leave the godly atmosphere in my home to chance.

Does all this mean that I have zero pain when I reflect on some of the issues from my past? No. Notice that all references to healing I have made in this chapter have been in the present as was Paul's statement, *"Forgetting* what is behind and *straining* toward what is ahead" (Phil. 3:13, emphasis added). This means that I am allowing God to heal me, that I am in the process of forgetting the past. And all this healing has empowered me to rewrite my story. Regardless of what has happened, I can move forward, a new creature in Christ.

Let the past sleep, but let it sleep in the sweet embrace of Christ, and let us go on into the invincible future with Him. Never let a sense of past failure defeat your next step.

—Oswald Chambers

Free to Influence

In Ps. 118, David writes, "In my anguish I cried to the LORD, and he answered by setting me free" (v. 5), and in Ps. 129, "They have greatly oppressed me from my youth, but they have not gained the victory over me. Plowmen have plowed my back and made their furrows long. But the LORD is righteous; he has cut me free from the cords of the wicked" (vv. 2-4). This is what God is in the business of doing—cutting us free from the cords of the wicked, the cords of the past, the cords of sin. If we're going to impact our homes and truly fulfill our spiritual role, we must allow God to cut the negative cords that have fed us lies and implant in us new cords that will feed us the presence of God.

When we are born into the world, the doctor cuts our

umbilical cord. We leave a confined space of relative comfort and burst forth to freedom. But what is our first response? We scream bloody murder! That freedom, all that space in which to move around, can be terrifying. If bondage has been a way of life, then freedom can sometimes appear scary. Nonetheless, God calls us to jump from our bondage into His arms and revel in the freedom. According to Oswald Chambers, "God does not give us overcoming life—He gives us life *as we overcome.* When the inspiration of God comes, and He says, 'Arise from the dead,' we have to get ourselves up. . . . If we will take the initiative to overcome, we will find that we have the inspiration of God, because He immediately gives us the power of life."[2]

In Matthew Jesus says to His disciples, "I tell you the truth, if you have faith as small as a mustard seed, you can say to this mountain, 'Move from here to there' and it will move. Nothing will be impossible for you" (17:20). Sometimes in our hearts we encounter mountains—mountains that trap us in the past, that stop us from moving into the present. But Jesus Christ tells us to have faith and tell those mountains to *move!* As the man with the outstretched hand, we must take some action. We have the faith to walk up to the base of those mountains, look them square in the face, and tell them they have no more space in our lives. At that point they have to move.

Do you want to be free from the cords of the past, free from the mountains that trap you, truly free to influence your home for God? Then by faith take the initiative and watch God give you the power of life overcoming, life renewed, life of powerful spiritual influence.

A wife of noble character who can find?
She is worth far more than rubies. . . .
She is clothed in fine linen and purple. . . .
She is clothed with strength and dignity.
—Prov. 31:10, 22, 25

Ruby "Am I's"

1. Am I allowing the past to prohibit my making an impact on the present?

   Evidence that you are: You often think something like "I could be more of a godly influence if this hadn't happened to me."

2. Am I embracing healing for my past?

   Evidence that you are: You have asked God to heal you and are allowing Him to embrace you daily.

3. Am I living in the past?

   Evidence that you are: Your thoughts are constantly bombarded with the painful situation from your past, and you can't seem to get over it.

4. Am I extending forgiveness toward those who have injured me?

   Evidence that you are: You fully realize that you have no right to harbor unforgiveness, because you have sinned against God just as that individual did who hurt you.

5. Am I rewriting my story?

   Evidence that you are: You no longer define yourself by your past.

6. Am I free to influence my family for Christ?

   Evidence that you are: You have allowed the Lord to cut the cords from the past, abandoned yourself to Him, and allowed Him to free you.

Ruby "Ifs"

If you are in the process of being healed:

- You have begun the journey of forgiving the person who injured you.
- You can talk about the issues that once gave you great pain.
- You feel no need to emotionally isolate yourself from your family and friends.
- You have followed Jesus' words to "get up" and "take your mat."
- You have rewritten your story.
- You are free to influence your home for Christ.

> *I have been reminded of your sincere faith, which first lived in your grandmother Lois and in your mother Eunice and, I am persuaded, now lives in you also. For this reason I remind you to fan into flame the gift of God, which is in you through the laying on of my hands.*
> —*2 Tim. 1:5-6*

~9~

Ruby Tips:
Practical Ways to Create a Godly Atmosphere in the Home

If you want to do all you can to fulfill your biblical role, then repeat in your home what happens at church:

1. **Open the Word of God.**

- *Privately read and memorize God's Word.*
- *Read the Word aloud with your family.*
- *Read the Word with your spouse.*
- *Meditate on the Word.*
- *Play pleasant Bible tapes while driving in the car.* My favorite is a collection of Bible verses with background music as well as the sounds of gentle rain, mountain streams, or ocean waves in the background.
- *Occasionally leave your Bible open in a high-traffic area in your home.* This tells your whole family that Mom has been reading the Word of God.
- *Place a large Bible in a high-visibility place of honor in your home.*

   2. Create a prayer habit.
   • *Pray privately.* Seek God with your whole heart.
   • *Pray with your family.* My husband is gone by the time the children and I start our day. I try to start their day with prayer. My husband closes the day with prayer during our regular family devotional time.
   • *Pray with your spouse.* As much as possible, have regular devotions with your spouse, even if it's once a week. Start the day in a "prayer hug."
   • *Pray as a group when guests or family are leaving.* Every time you have company, ask if you can pray together before departure.
   • *Always remember to pray for meals.* But never expect mealtime prayers to substitute for a prayer life.
   • *Create an organized prayer list and keep it updated.*
   • *Often tell your children, spouse, friends, and extended family that you're praying for them.*
   3. Enhance the atmosphere of your home through godly music.
   • *Play Christian music during family meals.*
   • *Turn off the television during family fun times, and turn on the worship music.*
   • *Play Christian music while you're in the car.*
   • *When your children are small, sing prayer choruses to them instead of lullabies.* (Nothing wrong with lullabies, but prayer choruses are more spiritually powerful.)
   • *Choose a variety of music.* This includes instrumentals, prayer choruses, upbeat new songs, as well as the old hymns of the Church. Young children love hymns, especially if they're sung at church as well. My two-year-old puckers her lips and sings her heart out.
   • *Choose music the whole family enjoys.* The family music experience should not be a drudgery for anyone. Create a mixture of different music styles in order to appeal to everyone's sense of worship, including yours.
   4. Fellowship.
   • *Spend time with your family as a unit.* Choose activities the whole family will enjoy.

- *Eat dinner together as a family as much as possible.*
- *Spend time one-on-one with each of your children.* Right now, that means a rocking chair and a book with my two-year-old. With my four-year-old, it means "our special day" when we go out and eat together.
- *Spend time one-on-one with your spouse.* "Kidnap" your husband for a weekend retreat. Plan regular "dates."

5. Encourage and praise your family.

- *When your children can read, hang up a dry-erase board in the dining room.* Assign one day per week or even a whole week for one family member. Daily write compliments and words of encouragement on the board for the assigned family member and read them aloud.
- *Tell your children they are exactly the kind of children you like, even if they're grown.*
- *Tell your husband you would chase him down and kiss his whole face if you had only just met him.* (Be prepared for chuckles.)
- *Daily ask the most positive force in the universe, our Heavenly Father, to create a positive attitude within you.*
- *Openly praise the Lord for every positive part of your life.*

6. Provide emotional and spiritual support.

- *If your child has a fear, concern, or illness, stop immediately for a hug and a brief moment of prayer.*
- *Create an emotionally safe environment in which your children can share spiritual and emotional concerns.* This comes through never mocking a child for his or her feelings.
- *Don't force a child into extra spiritual activities, but rather support the child in his or her endeavors.* For instance, I'm teaching Ps. 23 to my four-year-old. Last night I asked him if he was ready to work on it again. He was very tired and said no. I didn't push the issue. We'll pick it back up again later. But church attendance and participation in family devotions is a must and always will be.
- *Be ready to listen when your husband wants to share spiritual concerns.*

• *Try to understand your husband's emotional and physical needs, even if there are times when you really don't understand.* The effort is often a reward within itself.

7. Embrace your family.

• *Hug everybody in your family.*

• *Hug your spouse when he comes home.*

• *Hug your children repeatedly each day.*

• *Have regular family hugs.* Everyone stands in a circle and hugs everyone else. If you start this when children are small, you can continue it until they're adults.

• *Hug your family with your words, your expressions, and your unconditional love and approval.*

8. Be ready to take the offering.

• At church, we never fail to take an offering. The offering is an expression of our love for our Savior. Likewise, when you endeavor to create a godly atmosphere in your home, your family will naturally respond with an offering. In the offering they will return everything you've given to them and more, including unconditional love, praise, encouragement, spiritual richness, hugs, support, and fellowship.

A wife of noble character who can find? She is worth far more than rubies. . . . Her husband is respected at the city gate, where he takes his seat among the elders of the land. . . . Give her the reward she has earned, and let her works bring her praise at the city gate [where her husband takes his seat].

—Prov. 31:10, 23, 31

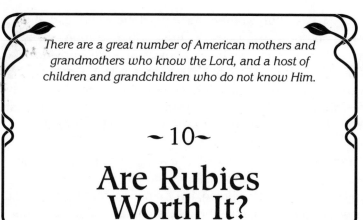

There are a great number of American mothers and grandmothers who know the Lord, and a host of children and grandchildren who do not know Him.

~10~

Are Rubies Worth It?

Now that you're in the closing pages of this book, you might be wondering if you really want to work this hard at your relationship with Jesus Christ and creating a godly atmosphere in your home. My answer is this: You really don't have a choice—that is, if you want to see your children and grandchildren saved. In *The Pastor's Playbook,* Stan Toler and Larry Gilbert share the following startling facts about the spiritual status of Americans:

Generation	Percentage Reached for Christ
Builders (Born before 1946)	65%
Boomers (Born between 1946 and 1964)	35%
Busters (Born between 1964 and 1977)	15%
Bridgers (Born between 1977 and 1994)	4%

Eighty-one percent of Christians accepted Christ *before* they were 20 years old, and the youngest busters and oldest bridgers are already older than 20. This indicates that, without some drastic changes, we stand very little chance of reaching much of the two younger generations for Christ.[1]

As Christian women, have we done all we can to influence our families for Jesus Christ? Have we done all we can to ensure that we have a powerful, earth-moving relationship with God that fills our homes with His presence? Have we made our families top priorities in our lives? Have we, with God as our helper, stopped wallowing in our pasts and started impacting our present for Jesus Christ?

Many topics discussed in this book could very easily be directed to men. For instance, if a man has dragons in his life, if a man refuses to make restitution, if a man doesn't have a powerful prayer life, if a man is materialistic, if a man is wallowing in his past, then the spiritual leadership of his home will be tainted. Given this truth, it would be very easy for a woman to say, "Why should I try to improve spiritually when my husband's not where *he's* supposed to be?" That question never exempts us from God's call to spiritual growth. It's Satan's trap to keep a woman from fulfilling her spiritual role in representing the Church to her family. Spiritual growth and fulfilling our God-ordained role are challenges that can be met only with continuous, determined effort.

This book might very easily turn into a five-year project for you. It's not a book a woman can read, put down, and easily implement the truths within a few weeks. So don't become frustrated when you have setbacks or feel that you've hit a plateau. Even during the writing of this book, I looked at my husband one evening and said, "I feel so inadequate to write on this subject because I don't feel I've got it all together myself." He looked at me, and with wisdom in his eyes he said, "Whether or not you feel you've got it all together doesn't alter truth. Truth is still truth." God's plan is for us to strive to be women of godly influence, regardless.

Considering all this, I recommend that after you've read through this book once, start over and slowly begin applying the truths one chapter at a time. Don't worry about any particular order of the chapters. For instance, if you successfully digest and apply chapter 1 and then feel the need to move to chapter 3, skip chapter 2 and come back to it later. Also, I recommend that you immediately begin applying as much of chapter 9 as possible.

Prov. 31:19 states, "In her hand she holds the distaff and grasps the spindle with her fingers." Notice the action of the verbs "holds" and "grasps." Also note the theme of weaving in this passage. These themes so underscore the role of a woman as the atmosphere of the home. A godly atmosphere involves the weaving of so many elements, and that task requires a woman who's willing to grasp the job and hold onto it for dear life.

Creating a godly atmosphere in the home will not happen with passive effort; it will happen only through determined weaving. And during all your weaving, remember—the wife really is the spirit of the home; the hand that rocks the cradle really does rule the world; beside every successful man, there really is a great woman; when Mama ain't happy, ain't nobody happy. Also remember that you really are worth more than rubies. Will you join me and take the challenge of radically filling your God-ordained role in your home? Yes, it *is* work. But it's the most important work you'll ever do.

A wife of noble character who can find?
She is worth far more than rubies. . . .
In her hand she holds the distaff
and grasps the spindle with her fingers.

—Prov. 31:10, 19

Notes

Chapter 1

1. *Church Around the World,* church bulletin insert published by Tyndale House, September 1998.

2. Gary Smalley and John Trent, *Love Is a Decision* (Dallas: Word, 1989), 46-47.

Chapter 2

1. John Maxwell, *The Winning Attitude* (Nashville: Thomas Nelson, 1993), 26-44, 159-60.

2. James Dobson, *What Wives Wish Their Husbands Knew About Women* (Wheaton, Ill.: Tyndale House, 1975), 15-18.

3. Wilbur Glenn Williams, "Baal Worship: The Worship of Sexuality Is Not Just a Modern Phenomena," *Illustrated Bible Life* (Dec./Jan./Feb. 1998-99): 60-62.

Chapter 3

1. William Longstaff, "Take Time to Be Holy" in *Worship in Song* (Kansas City: Lillenas Publishing Company, 1972), 33.

Chapter 4

1. Oswald Chambers, *My Utmost for His Highest,* n.p., January 22 devotional.

2. Ibid., June 27 devotional.

3. Stan Toler, interview, January 28, 1998.

Chapter 5

1. J. Otis and Gail Ledbetter, "The Pleasures of Respect," in *Family Fragrance: Practical, Intentional Ways to Fill Your Home with the Aroma of Love* (Colorado Springs: Chariot Victor, 1998), 48-72.

2. Judy Cornelia Pearson and Paul Edward Nelson, *Understanding and Sharing* (Dubuque, Iowa: William C. Brown, 1979), 50.

Chapter 6

1. Nathaniel Hawthorne, "Rappaccini's Daughter," in *The Norton Anthology of American Literature,* 3rd ed., ed. Nina Baym et al. (New York: Norton, 1979), 1:1143-62.

2. Ibid., 1:1160.

3. *Mother Teresa: A Simple Path,* comp. Lucinda Vardey (New York: Ballantine, 1995), 99.

4. Bernard of Clairvaux, "On the Love of God," in *Late Medieval Mysticism,* ed. Ray Petry (Philadelphia: Westminster Press, 1957), 59.

5. John Wesley Wright, "Mammon—a Word Study," in *Illustrated Bible Life,* vol. 21, No. 3. (March-April-May 1998), 13.

6. Ibid.

7. Quoted in *Mother Teresa,* 46.

8. Ibid., 45.

9. Alan Harkey, interview, April 2, 1998.

10. Ibid.

11. Ibid.

12. Patsy Clairmont, "Lookin' Good," in *God Uses Cracked Pots* (Colorado Springs: Focus on the Family, 1991), 3-5.

13. Willard F. Harley Jr., *His Needs, Her Needs: Building an Affair-Proof Marriage* (Grand Rapids: Revell, 1986), 3.

Chapter 7

1. James Dobson, *What Wives Wish Their Husbands Knew About Women* (Wheaton, Ill.: Tyndale, 1975), 25.

2. Ibid.

3. Ibid., 57.

Chapter 8

1. Jerry Hull and Larry Hull, *Fully Alive: Discovering the Adventure of Healthy and Holy Living* (Kansas City: Beacon Hill Press of Kansas City, 1998), 48.

2. Chambers, *My Utmost for His Highest,* n.p., February 16 devotional.

Chapter 10

1. Stan Toler and Larry Gilbert, *The Pastor's Playbook* (Kansas City: Beacon Hill Press of Kansas City, 2000), chap. 1.

Works Cited

Chambers, Oswald. *My Utmost for His Highest.*

Church Around the World, church bulletin insert published by Tyndale House. September 1998.

Bernard of Clairvaux. "On the Love of God," in *Late Medieval Mysticism,* ed. Ray Petry. Philadelphia: Westminster Press, 1957.

Clairmont, Patsy. "Lookin' Good" in *God Uses Cracked Pots.* Colorado Springs: Focus on the Family, 1991.

Dobson, James. *What Wives Wish Their Husbands Knew About Women.* Wheaton, Ill.: Tyndale House, 1975.

Harkey, Alan. Interview, April 2, 1998.

Harley, Willard F., Jr. *His Needs, Her Needs: Building an Affair-Proof Marriage.* Grand Rapids: Revell, 1986.

Hawthorne, Nathaniel. "Rappaccini's Daughter" in *The Norton Anthology of American Literature,* 3rd ed., ed. Nina Baym et al. New York: Norton, 1979.

Hull, Jerry, and Larry Hull. *Fully Alive: Discovering the Adventure of Healthy and Holy Living.* Kansas City: Beacon Hill Press of Kansas City, 1998.

Ledbetter, J. Otis and Gail. *Family Fragrance: Practical, Intentional Ways to Fill Your Home with the Aroma of Love.* Colorado Springs: Chariot Victor, 1998.

Maxwell, John. *The Winning Attitude.* Nashville: Thomas Nelson, 1993.

Minamede, Elaine. "Overcommitted Moms: Workaholics at Home" in *Focus on the Family* (February 1999): 6-7.

Mother Teresa: A Simple Path, comp. Lucinda Vardey. New York: Ballantine, 1995.

Pearson, Judy Cornelia, and Paul Edward Nelson. *Understanding and Sharing.* Dubuque, Iowa: William C. Brown, 1979.

Smalley, Gary, and John Trent. *Love Is a Decision.* Dallas: Word, 1989.

Toler, Stan. Interview, January 28, 1998.

Toler, Stan, and Larry Gilbert. *The Pastor's Playbook.* Kansas City: Beacon Hill Press of Kansas City, 2000.

Williams, Wilbur Glenn. "Baal Worship: The Worship of Sexuality Is Not Just a Modern Phenomena" in *Illustrated Bible Life* 22, No. 2 (December/January/February 1998-99).

Worship in Song. Kansas City: Lillenas Publishing Company, 1972.

Wright, John Wesley. "Mammon—a Word Study" in *Illustrated Bible Life* 21, No. 3 (March/April/May 1998).